FROM DIVORCE TO DELIVERANCE…

Divorce Doesn't (Have to) Mean Devastation!

— ♥ —

Wisdom from the Judge on

Surviving Divorce Legally & Emotionally

With Your Sanity, Stability, & Spirit Intact!

BY RONIQUE BASTINE ROBINSON

Cover Design: Wendy Davis

Interior Design: Wendy Davis

ISBN: **0692276807**
ISBN 13: **9780692276808**

DEDICATION

This book is dedicated to my family for allowing me to pursue my love of the law and to my clients for allowing me to share in their personal journeys.

ACKNOWLEDGEMENTS

I would like to first thank my Lord and Savior Jesus Christ for blessing me abundantly and allowing me to use my gifts to bless others. Thank you to my clients for sharing their stories, their pains, their joys and their triumphs.

Also, a big thanks to my encouragers, Dr. Press Robinson and Dr. Dana Smith for their invaluable input, watchful eyes, and listening ears. My sincere appreciation also goes out to my pastor Dr. Marcus D. Cosby, Senior Pastor of Wheeler Avenue Baptist Church and Dr. Howard John Wesley, Sr., Senior Pastor of Alfred Street Baptist Church for their guidance and assistance with helping me to find scriptures that would encourage the grieving heart and heal the wounded soul. Thank you to Rev. William Alexander Lawson, Pastor Emeritus of Wheeler Avenue Baptist Church, for being my spiritual guide and my shining example. I am grateful that he made himself available every single time I called, and my appreciation for his love and wisdom over the years is immeasurable.

Lastly, I'd like to thank my husband and my children for sacrificing their time and energy to allow me the opportunity to pursue my dream of writing this book.

Contents

INTRODUCTION

Not *Me*, God! Not *Now*!

If people were to observe you from across the room as you leafed through the pages of this book at this very moment, they might look at you and think that everything was perfect. After all, you look pleasant and normal enough. What they would not know just by looking at you is that you've masterfully managed to hide the confusion, grief, heartbreak, despair, and gut-wrenching pain that only someone who has experienced the failure of a significant relationship can relate to. *God, please! This can't be happening to me. Not to me! Not now!*

If you could really act out the way that you feel at the moment, you would just fall to the ground, curl up and cry – that is, if you have any tears left. You've shed more tears since you realized that you were on the brink of this situation than you've probably ever shed in your life. Sometimes you cry without even thinking about it; you're just walking around handling your business, and then all of a sudden, you feel hot tears falling from your eyes. They remind you that while your mind was focused on other things at the moment, your heart has not forgotten the current devastation of your life. It reacts out of the truth of your circumstances, even when you manage to distract your mind with other things. What's the truth? You are in the midst of a season of all-out, full-on, bona fide grief and despair, and although you are not an extremist, you wonder if there will ever come a day when you feel normal again.

Yes, you put up a good front because you have to, but the truth is that you are in the midst of dealing with what is perhaps the biggest disappointment of your life. You feel like a total failure to yourself and your family, and you feel like a disappointment to those around you. After all of your initial talk about being in love, this being the one for you, and "until death do us part", after all of the wedding gifts, anniversary celebrations, the "my spouse is a true gift from God", and the public displays of affection that made you seem like you were the perfect couple with the happy life, everything has come crashing down around you. If it was not your choice to initiate the divorce, take all of these feelings and multiply them by 100. Yes, I know. It feels just that bad. It's a wonder you can even function. Quite possibly, the pain you feel is so intense that even though you know emotions are not tangible, you would swear they are moving around inside causing the type of physical pain that makes you double over and cry out in anguish. It's hard to manage this way. If your situation is *really* fresh, you're almost certainly in tears at this point as you read; but keep reading, because hope is ahead.

The good news is that though these feelings flood your soul every day, you do *at least* manage to get up and pull yourself together – even if it is only on the outside. I know, your mind is in a fog, and though you're walking around and interacting with people, it takes an enormous amount of energy just to focus. I know, even though it appears that you are listening and paying attention to your boss, your co-workers, and even your children if you have any, you can barely manage to connect two plus two. Heck, you can barely convince your brain to help you get up, dress and feed yourself; that is, if you are eating anything at all these days. I know, you drive from point A to point B and yet remember nothing about the trip or how you got there. I know your mind is so off that you're likely to put salt in your coffee instead of sugar and lose the remote control, only to discover days later you placed it in the freezer. You forget what you were looking for when you went into the bedroom, and you can't remember the point you were making mid-sentence. I know all about the fog that takes over the brain when you go through periods of extreme grief like this – the kind that causes you to walk around like a zombie in a daze.

You try to cope by having a drink, but it just makes you sadder and the tears flow more freely. You try to watch your favorite comedy to get a laugh, but nothing is funny. You try to distract yourself with a crime drama or reality TV but realize that your life is an even bigger train wreck than the semi-fictitious drama unfolding before you on the screen. You try to socialize and hang out with your friends – at their request, because they are worried about your constant isolation – but they soon grow tired of hearing you ask "*Why*" questions about your soon-to-be ex-spouse that cannot be answered by anyone but your soon-to-be ex-spouse and are becoming impatient when all you want to do is talk about your relationship. They ask, "Can't we talk about something else?" You try to pray and talk to God, but you feel no connection. All you feel is empty and spent.

No one from the outside would guess that you spend the vast majority of your days preoccupied with trying to figure out how you ended up where you are, asking yourself question after question. Why did this have to happen? Why didn't I see this coming? Why couldn't we make it work? How did we get here? Is it really too late to turn things around? Is there anything else I could have done to prevent this? What is the *real* reason my spouse wants to leave? Is my spouse in love with someone else? Am I really *that* undesirable? When did we fall out of love? Did my spouse ever *really* love me?

If you're beyond the point of asking these types of questions, it is likely that you've moved on to a whole different set of questions. Where am I going to live? Is my spouse going to try to take everything from me? Should I try to take all I can first? Is this divorce going to be ugly? Who will get to keep the kids? How am I going to afford the legal fees? Will my friends still want to associate with me? What will the people at my job and church members think? Will anyone want me after this? Will I be alone for the rest of my life? And these are the just the questions you ask during the day.

When night comes, and you are in the dark safe privacy of your own room, you take off the mask, let your defenses down, and allow the floodgate to open, giving way to a roaring rapid of more questions, tears, screams into the pillow and feelings of anger, rejection, resentment, rage, fury, sorrow, desperation, and sadness – oh God, the sadness – that you've been holding in all day. The memories of your spouse that you once held as dear recollections of a love story that would go on forever now haunt you; you shake your head as they come to mind, wondering if it was all a lie.

If this was one of the nights that you had to take a sleeping pill to get a few hours of rest before facing the world the next day, you gaze at the ceiling, praying that it would take effect and put you out of your misery for the night. If you listened to your friend who told you not to start taking those pills "because you could get hooked on them, and you don't want to have to deal with that," sleep may take a little longer. You don't even know at what point you fell asleep; you are just grateful that you were actually able to sleep on this night.

At this point, you might be saying to yourself, "This judge *had* to have gone through a divorce to know exactly what I'm feeling at this level." However, with this presumption, you are only half-correct. Yes, I have lived through divorce, but it was not mine. I lived through the divorce of my parents, I have lived through the divorces of very close dear friends, and I lived through divorce as an attorney representing clients who were experiencing this devastation first-hand. One thing that has made me a top-rated attorney and a well-respected judge over the past 20 years is also what makes me a really good friend: I listen. I hold onto every word and hear every word that people speak to me. In fact, I listen so closely that sometimes, I begin to feel deep in my emotions what the other person is expressing with words. This is why I can empathize so closely with those going through divorce.

When my clients tell me the deepest, darkest, ugliest secrets of their situations, they know that I must hold everything they tell me in the strictest of confidence; I must abide by attorney-client privilege and not share what they have said with anyone. People seem to feel a certain sense of freedom to come clean about things – even things unrelated to the legal matter I am representing – when they know that it cannot be repeated. This is no wonder, because the Bible says that open confession is good for the soul. However, it is not only my clients that come clean out of an expectation of attorney-client privilege; my friends do as well. Now, mind you, attorney-client privilege does not apply to matters discussed between friends. They just assume that because I am an attorney, I have to keep all of their secrets to myself. In any case, I don't mind; I just go with it! As a result, my friends and associates have nicknamed me "The Keeper of Secrets", a title that I proudly wear, because under no circumstances have I ever violated their confidentiality.

One of the benefits of being a "vault" that guards secrets is that when people, particularly those who are in the throes of divorce, toss their filters aside and open up to engage in a no-hold-barred conversation about their experiences, if you listen closely, you learn *a lot*. A *whole* lot! You learn that regardless of where people are from, the color of their skin, where they went to school or how much money they make, the pain and grief of divorce are the same for everyone. The fears are the same, the questions are the same, and the hope for a day to come when they will feel normal and happy – to be able to laugh again, even if only for a few minutes – is the same.

Both my personal experiences and my professional legal career, coupled with a strong spiritual relationship with my Creator, have earned me a wealth of knowledge about how to survive the tragedy of divorce. And yes, divorce is just that: a tragedy. Some counselors have described it as an experience worse than living through the actual physical death of a spouse. They describe it this way because the ex-spouse is no longer a part of your life but a walking, breathing reminder of the death of the relationship. As such, there is no finality. However, just as I know the intricacies of the tragedy of divorce, I know the process of getting through it, both emotionally and legally. I have walked with person after person through the experience, and I have seen what works and what does not work, again, both emotionally and legally. Although there is no real "right way" to go through such a difficult and emotional storm, I have witnessed first-hand the outcomes of those who did it the wise way as well as watched those who did things the foolish way. Parties in both scenarios have stood before my bench as I rendered verdicts in the courtroom. Trust me. Do it the wise way.

My courtroom is often occupied by ex-spouses being brought up on charges for a wide variety of reasons that could have been easily avoided if they had only received some sound help and guidance in going through their process. As I watch them being brought up on charges for slashing their ex's tires, disturbing the peace at their ex's home, physically fighting with their ex, or acting out some other bitterness, anger, or rage-related behavior at the expense of their ex-spouse, I can only shake my head. However, I do not do so for the cause of judging them. Instead, I do so because I know that they need help. There is so little practical, relevant help available to people in these situations that can show them how to navigate the process of gracefully dissolving a relationship with a spouse, both emotionally and legally. This book is my effort to help.

As you read this book, you might be at one of several different stages. You might have had "the dreaded conversation" with your partner and decided that the best way to go is to dissolve the marriage, but you are still living with one another – perhaps even still sharing the same bed. You might have had "the dreaded conversation" with your spouse and couldn't bear the agony of looking at your future ex, so you are now living apart as the process begins. You might be further on in the process, having been separated for a little while as each of you waits for the other's next move. If you're not the one who acts first, you're probably the one wondering, "Is my partner really going to file papers against me? Are we really going to do this? I'm going to wait and see." If you are spiritual, you might be separated, but praying like you've never prayed before for God to give you a miracle of reconciliation, because you know that there is nothing too hard for Him. You might be in a position in which you are already deep into the process, scheduling meetings with mediators, arbitrators and attorneys and going to court dates as you battle the person you once loved with all of your heart to maintain possession of the things that mean the most to you. Or, it might all be over. You might be finally, completely and legally divorced, wondering how to go on with your life. What's the next move? You truly cannot figure out where to go from here.

As a judge, many people expect me to be *naturally* wise; they expect for me to be able to tell them exactly what to do for practically every situation in their lives, because after all... I'm a judge! However, I have the good fortune of understanding something that many others do not: true wisdom comes from above – from God! As a woman of faith, I lean and depend on God and His word in the Bible for the wisdom to know what to do and how to do it. When I need wisdom, guidance, and direction, I seek Him through reading scriptures and through prayer, and He always speaks to me with exactly what I need at the time. Without His wisdom, which is pure, peace-loving, considerate, submissive, full of mercy and good fruit, impartial and sincere (James 3:13-18), I would be *completely* lost!

Divorce is a situation in which you are going to need a lot of access to things that only God can offer: wisdom, direction, love, healing, and joy, just to name a few. I am reminded of a story in the Bible that fully encompasses this concept to help you understand just how much He desires to keep you in the midst of such a hard transition. The context of this Bible story is one of national transition in which the current king of Israel, Saul, has lost his anointing because he was disobedient to God. Therefore, God needed to replace him. God sends one of His prophets, Samuel, to seek out and anoint the next young man who would be king: David. However, Saul was still in office, and he was a fierce king. What would he do if he heard about Samuel anointing another king behind his back? Thus, Samuel was concerned and needed God's encouragement, direction, and guidance; the outcome of his life depended on God's wisdom! The passage from 1 Samuel 16:1-4 says:

Verse 1: *The LORD said to Samuel, "How long will you mourn for Saul, since I have rejected him as king over Israel? Fill your horn with oil and be on your way; I am sending you to Jesse of Bethlehem. I have chosen one of his sons to be king."*

Verse 2: *But Samuel said, "How can I go? If Saul hears about it, he will kill me."*

The LORD said, "Take a heifer with you and say, 'I have come to sacrifice to the LORD.'

Verse 3: *Invite Jesse to the sacrifice, and I will show you what to do. You are to anoint for me the one I indicate."*

Verse 4: *Samuel did what the LORD said. When he arrived at Bethlehem, the elders of the town trembled when they met him. They asked, "Do you come in peace?"*

In verse 1, we see God asking Samuel how long he would mourn for Saul, the one whom God rejected. In your own relationship, could it be that God has allowed the break-up of your marriage because He has something better for you? Could it be that where He is taking you in life, in ministry, in your relationship with Him, and in your destiny, you would be unable to go with your current relationship? Could it be that the relationship was doing you and/or your children so much harm that God allowed it to dissolve to protect you spiritually, emotionally, and even physically? Could it be that even though God gave you warning after warning about your spouse before you got married, and you got married anyway because you wanted the person so badly, but He was only going to allow you to be out of His will for so long before He allowed it to fail?

If God has "rejected" your spouse, it has to be for a really good reason. You might not realize what the reason is until a year or two from now, or you might not realize the reason until you get to eternity. However, just know that as painful as this situation is, it will work together for your good in the future (Romans 8:28). In light of this understanding, God is asking you how long you will mourn for that which *He Himself* has rejected! Trust me: if God doesn't want something or someone in your life, you shouldn't either. In His all-knowingness, He knows so much more about what is happening in the background than we do, and He always knows best! Just as God told Samuel to fill his horn of oil and be on his way, God is telling you to trust Him by making preparation for your future and being on your way. It's time to stop mourning the past and to set out on your journey for a greater future, because He has so much more in store for you! Take note that I am not saying that a failed marriage is God's will. It is not His will for us to fail, but if He has allowed it by not stopping it with His sovereign power, we must accept what He allows. Divorce is never His will, but He does offer comfort and peace for those who are divorced.

In verse 2, we see Samuel questioning God, who has just told him to stop worrying about Saul and to move forward. He asks God, *"How can I go? If Saul hears about it, he will kill me."* When we are overly concerned about people who are now a part of our past, we can have a hard time hearing what God is saying to us. God, the Creator of the universe, the maker of all men, the One with the exclusive ability to speak life or death, the One who is all-seeing, all-knowing, all-powerful – the sovereign, mighty King – has just given Samuel direction on how to proceed. Yet, Samuel dares to question God's directions because of what another *man* might do. A mortal man whom *God* created. A man to whom *God* could speak a word to and cause to lay down and die! What a mere man might be able to do to us is no match for God! Therefore, if God gives you direction to do something, the last thing that you should consider is what man might do to you because you were obedient to Him.

I see this happen over and over again when handling divorce cases. I will pray for wisdom and tell my clients to pray for wisdom about how to proceed in the divorce case. Then, God will answer and we will have our marching orders about how to act or respond to a particular action. However, my clients will often have a tendency to second guess themselves, asking, "Wait! I can't do that! If I do this, what will my spouse think? Won't my spouse be mad at me? My spouse will be so angry that he/she will want to kill me!" My clients fear many things that their spouses can do to them in a divorce case, from seeking retribution, to taking things from them and causing them great loss, to not wanting to get back together with them – if there was ever even a chance of this happening. It is then that I have to remind them that we sought the Lord for the answers, and He told us how to proceed. Therefore, they have no need to worry about what someone else – especially someone who is now a part of their past – will do to them. When you are simply following the Lord's counsel, whatever your spouse might feel as a result of your obedience is inconsequential. Your job is to simply walk in obedience to Him, and His job is to take care of you – and to handle your spouse!

Next, in verse 3, God says, *Invite Jesse to the sacrifice, and I will show you what to do. You are to anoint for me the one I indicate.* Here, we see that after God has spoken a direction to Samuel on where to go, He now gives him a clear directive on what to do. When you are in a right relationship with God and seek His wisdom, He will not only give you a wise plan, but He will give you protection from your spouse as you execute that plan. Again, when you are walking in obedience to God, fear not what man can do to you, even in the courtroom!

Finally, in verse 4, we see that *Samuel did what the LORD said.* He was obedient to God and walked out the wise plan that the Lord gave him. As a result, he found the young shepherd boy named David and anointed him as king. Eventually, after much struggle during the transition, David would be king! This is a lesson to us that out of our obedience comes God's plan for our lives even when there is struggle in the transition. Out of Samuel's obedience to God's wisdom came the anointing of David, who would go on to be the greatest king that ever reigned in Israel. What will come out of your obedience to God's wisdom? The Father will anoint your next steps if you are obedient to His wisdom, His will, and His directions. If you are obedient to God and in right relationship with Him, you will be able to hear His voice of guidance!

In the chapters that follow, I am going to pull from everything I know legally, ethically, psychologically, and spiritually to help you in your process, whether you are about to embark on the journey to divorce, in the middle of the process, or at the final end trying to figure out which path to take to put your life back together again. In order to navigate the complex legal process ahead, you need to get to a healthy mental state that will allow you to function clearly and take care of your business, and I want to help lead you there. It is my goal to help you figure out where you are emotionally, why you are feeling what you are feeling, and how to get to a better place of spiritual wellness and wholeness. I'm going to do all I can to help you gain a new perspective of life, of love, and of what your future can be. I will show you how relying on God as you go through a process like this can be the absolute best thing you've ever done, because it is the only way to survive something so tragic with your sanity intact; I see a *striking* difference between the outcomes of my friends and clients who go through divorce hand-in-hand with God and those who try to brave the storm alone. Finally, I will equip you with tools and wisdom that you need to win and come out healed – or at least well on your way to it – and whole on the other side.

If you will trust me to walk with you through this process, by the end of it, I guarantee that you will be less fearful, less bitter, more understanding, more at peace, more sane, and in a much better position to set out to establish the future that you desire for yourself. As I write this book, I do not write it alone; I pray through every aspect of it and ask God to show me what to say and how to say it so that these words will not only comfort and encourage, but empower and equip people for wholeness and wellness. If I've done my job, at the end of this book, you will better understand the process of divorce – legally and emotionally – you will have a new sense of hope and expectation, and you will be at a place where your faith will be stronger than ever. Thank you for allowing me the privilege of accompanying you on your journey *From Divorce to Deliverance*.

A Prayer for Direction…

Before moving on to the next chapter, pray this prayer aloud:

God, I am in the midst of one of the most difficult and challenging situations in my life, and I am seeking Your wisdom, guidance, and direction for how to move forward. I pray that as I read the pages of this book that you would speak to me in a way that I can clearly hear and understand. Help me to embrace what You tell me to do and not operate out of my own fleshly wisdom. Help me to have the obedience and courage to trust in You with all of my heart and lean not on my own understanding. Help me to acknowledge You in every decision that I make, every action I take, and every resolve I establish, knowing that you will direct my path. I trust You with my life, and I am depending on You to make it through this season.

Lead me through it, Lord, and I will follow You. Amen!

CHAPTER ONE

What to Expect When You're Expecting
– to Divorce

Embarking upon the journey of divorce can be a very scary thing, primarily because of the unknowns surrounding it. Sure, you've seen your favorite stars on television go through very public divorces, and you've even seen people that you actually know go through divorces, so you are familiar with the *concept* of it. You, like many others, probably have a surface understanding of it like the general population: two people hire attorneys who type up and file lots of papers, fight it out in court, and help you split up your possessions with your ex-spouse, so that in the end, you are no longer married and you live in separate homes.

However, what *exactly* is entailed in the process of divorce? What is the difference between a petitioner and a respondent, and which are you? What is a discovery period? What is an affidavit? How do you determine who gets what? What determines how much child support a parent will receive?

How can you get alimony? Then, there's one of the most popular questions: How much is this going to *cost* me?

Before you get started or jump into the divorce process, it's important to get educated on what to expect when you are expecting to go through a divorce. Nothing ensures a successful outcome in the legal battle of divorce more than an informed client.

Knowing what to expect when you begin the process of divorce will make you less afraid, less intimidated, and less anxious, while at the same time making you more confident, more settled, and more prepared for whatever happens during your divorce journey.

This chapter is designed to introduce you to a summary of what to expect during the process of divorce from a legal standpoint. The legalities surrounding divorce can range from very simple to quite complex; it all depends upon your individual situation. Some divorce logistics will be just about the same wherever you go, while others will vary or differ from state to state. In any case, based upon my decades of work in the legal field, I can give you a broad overview of what to expect when you are expecting to divorce with as little "legal-ese" as possible so as not to further confuse you on what is an already confusing topic of conversation.

Step 1:
Be Clear about Your True Desire:
Divorce or Reconciliation?

Time to Have an Honest Conversation with Yourself

Whether you have already discussed the option of divorce with your partner or you are just silently considering all of your options, the very first step in the process is to decide upon what you really want. You might have thought that the first step in the divorce process would have been to have a conversation with an attorney, but you are quite wrong. The truth is, the very first conversation that you should have when embarking upon a divorce is a very transparent one with yourself. It all begins with this question: What do *I really* want?

Identifying what you want – first and foremost – is a critical initial step in the process. Why? Because when you approach an attorney, one of the first questions the attorney is programmed to ask is, "What do you want?" If you have not taken the time to seriously think through this important question, you will be wasting valuable time – and money – when you approach an attorney.

Here's a primary first lesson for you to remember when working with an attorney: time is money. The more time you spend in your attorney's office, on your attorney's phone, or engaged in talking things through with your attorney, the more money you will be shelling out. Therefore, do as much thinking and working through things as you can before you engage an attorney. You will find that it really pays off – financially, mentally, and emotionally – to think through everything before you set the legal process in motion.

Sometimes, once people sit down and have a conversation with themselves to carefully consider what they want, they experience a revelation: *What I really want is reconciliation!* Arriving at this conclusion will have a big effect on how you approach your legal situation. There are several approaches to take in this situation.

Reconciliation Plan A: Just Ask for It

In this reconciliation approach, let your partner know that it is time to have a serious talk. Set aside some time when you are both calm and neutral (if such a state can even be achieved at this point), and have the conversation in a place that is free from distraction; the only thing you need to focus on right now is each other. Then, lay everything on the table.

Share your love for your partner, your hopes and dreams for your relationship, and your acceptance of your partner for who he or she really is. Talk about the time and energy that you have invested into the relationship, the family and life that you have built together, and how much of a shame it would be to throw this all away. Offer forgiveness for what your partner has done to you, and ask to be forgiven for your role in making the relationship what it now is. Propose getting help in the form of third-party counseling or coaching. With as much sincere humility as you can muster, ask for a reconciliation of the relationship.

Reconciliation Plan B: Try Some Time Apart in Separation

Sometimes, having a heartfelt conversation is not enough to spur your partner towards reconciliation; sometimes it takes something more impacting to accomplish such results. Sometimes, it takes something that alters your partner's life and daily routine to such an extent that the prospect of living without you and the family that you have built together becomes a tangible reality. When your partner wakes up without you, doesn't have someone to help out with the house or the kids, doesn't have someone to come home to, doesn't have someone to share the highs and lows of

3

the workday with, and no longer shares a life and intimacy with the one who played the role of "best friend" for years, the impact of this level of separation alone can bring about a desire to reconcile.

There is an old adage that says, "You don't know what you got until it's gone." This one is a close cousin to, "You don't miss your water until your well runs dry." Then there is yet another one that says, "Absence makes the heart grow fonder." The underlying sentiment behind each of these sayings is the same: you don't realize how much you have taken someone for granted until you have to live without them, and it is only then that you appreciate them more than ever and recognize that you don't *want* to live without them.

Sometimes, spending an extended amount of time apart from you is enough to bring your partner to this point. I've seen it several times in cases with my clients. The conversation asking for reconciliation did not work; there was too much history, too much baggage, too many hurt feelings, and too many walls built up around the spouse's heart to be able to penetrate it with mere conversation. Not willing to throw in the towel yet, one of my clients felt like it was time to take more drastic action to save the relationship; since her partner did not respond to reconciliation, she asked for a separation.

I should explain here that there are two types of separation: Contractual Separation and Legal Separation. Different states observe different types of separation. For example, the state of Texas does not have Legal Separation, only Contractual Separation.

Contractual Separation usually occurs when one member of the couple moves out of the home that they share together. This might mean moving in with a friend or a relative, into another property that the couple owns, or even renting a new apartment and living alone. Both parties in the couple work together to decide the terms of the separation like visitation with the children, how the primary household's bills will be paid, how monies in a joint bank account will be spent, how much can be spent on joint credit cards, etc.

Usually, when a couple decides to contractually separate, it can be for various reasons, one of which is because one or both parties feel like spending some time alone to "air out", "cool down", and get themselves together will give them a chance at coming together and developing a stronger, more fulfilling marriage. There is no official time period governing the length of the separation; the couple most often maintains some level of communication, and depending upon how things are going after a certain length of time, they will either stay happily separated, recognize how much they love each other and reconcile, or move ahead with filing for divorce if things just cannot be worked out between them.

Legal Separation is a separation with terms that are defined by a court of law. While in an informal separation, both parties of the couple work together to determine how issues like visitation, care of the primary household, bank accounts, etc. will be handled, a legal separation is a formal separation with directives that can be enforced by the law.

For example, in an informal separation, a couple can decide to still direct deposit their paychecks into the same account, and after the bills are paid, they can each withdraw a certain amount of spending money for themselves. If one person withdraws more than what was agreed upon, the only thing that the other party can do is get angry. However, if this same arrangement was stipulated by the courts in a legal separation and one party violated it, that person would be in contempt of court. The consequence: potential jail time! Therefore, be careful to know what is and is not permissible when dealing with legal separation, and take all terms that are outlined by the court seriously!

One or both parties will usually choose to go through a legal separation if it is available in their state and there is more at stake in the relationship. For example, if you and your partner have a trust-compromised relationship and you simply cannot trust your partner to not touch the last $25,000 that you have left in your joint savings account (no matter how many times you hear, "I promise on the *bible* I won't touch it again!"), your interests would be better protected by going the legal separation route. In this case, the judge could stipulate that neither of you is legally able to touch it without obtaining certain permissions that are outlined by the court.

Like contractual separation, a legal separation is designed to give both parties in a couple some time to live apart from one another with hopes of them realizing that life apart is not what they want; thus, they reconcile. Separation has been proven effective in many, many cases, so while it may not lead to optimal results for you, it does work for others. In fact, it is so effective that in some states, before the court will grant you a divorce, it requires a legal separation for up to one year!

The time period surrounding how long a legal separation will last depends upon the circumstances surrounding it. If the separation is court-mandated before a divorce can be granted, the court will stipulate that the couple has to be legally separated for some prescribed period of time. In cases where two people decide to contractually separate on their own, there are no set time periods for the separation. If the parties have filed for divorce and have contractually agreed to separate, the automated court system may generate a trial date, which will spur them to make a decision by a certain deadline, or they can ask for more time. If they have not filed for divorce with the court, then the husband and wife can decide if and when they want to move forward with the process of divorce. I know one couple that was separated for 14 years before they reconciled, never having filed for a divorce with the court. While this is not typical, it is certainly an example of how the process can work, even if it takes years!

Reconciliation Plan C: File for Divorce

If Plan A and Plan B did not work, actually filing for divorce may be your last ditch effort to get your partner's attention. It is not uncommon for people to actually file for divorce to drive home the point of how serious they are about leaving the relationship. Sometimes, this is exactly what it takes to shake up their spouse to the point that he or she says, "My spouse is really serious! I'd better straighten up and fly right, or I'm going to lose the family and the life that I love!" Just by filing for divorce, you might achieve your desired outcome of reconciliation. At this point, you can notify your attorney to drop the case. Mission accomplished.

However, for every case that works out so ideally, there are several other clients that desire reconciliation and do not achieve it by filing for divorce. If your partner does not waver after being served with divorce papers, it looks like you'll actually be going through with the divorce. You've exhausted all of your options, and now, it's time to get down to business. Pull out your pen and paper, and start making your list of demands, because there is much to be gained and lost in the battle.

A Word to the Wise...

If you are filing for divorce to get your partner's attention with the hopes of reconciliation, let your attorney know up front! The way attorneys approach the case of a client who wants reconciliation is quite different from the way they will approach the case of a client who is ready to go to all-out war! Be very clear and up front from the very beginning so that you and your attorney stay on the same page.

Step 2:
Decide What You Want Out of the Divorce

Do the Legwork: Spend Time Deciding What YOU Want!

Now that you have made a final decision about moving ahead with a divorce, it is time to move the "What do I really want?" conversation a step further. This time, the decision about what you really want centers on what you desire to take out of the marriage. Again, the primary question an attorney will ask you when you sit down for your first consultation is "What do you want?" If you choose to conduct this exercise sitting in your attorney's office, just know you are being charged for it one way or another.

Remember: their time is your money!

In an effort to maximize your dollar, do all of the prep work you can before going to your attorney. Instead of sitting in your attorney's office trying to figure out if you want the dog, the new custom-built barbecue smoker, or the time share in Florida with the high annual maintenance fees, think through these things beforehand. Then, when you finally do approach your attorney, present your carefully-constructed list of demands. Doing so will not only save you time and money, but it will give you the reassurance that you have taken all of the time you needed to think through things and consider all of your options. The last thing you want is to feel rushed to decide such an important matter.

Leave <u>Nothing</u> on the Marital Estate Table!

When you are engaged in the process of trying to figure out what you want, leave nothing on the table! Divorce is all about give and take, so while most of the things on the table are things that you will want to take (especially if you feel wronged by your spouse), there will also be things that you will inevitably have to give. Nonetheless, do not be afraid to ask for everything you could possibly want from the marital estate. *Marital estate* includes all of the property that you have acquired together during the time you were married. *Everything* means *everything*, all the way down to the forks, knives, gaming consoles and household plants!

If you do not ask for something, your attorney will not know to include it in your request, and the judge will not know to grant it to you. Therefore, take time to make your list and review it several times to make sure any and everything you want is included. Do not be afraid to be too specific; your attorney will let you know if you've crossed over the line into too much detail. If, during the divorce process, you remember something you have left off of your list of demands, be sure to tell your attorney immediately so it can be included on your lists of requests in court!

Some people will completely skip the step of asking for part of the marital estate's property altogether; they are so finished with the relationship and so ready to get out that they say, "You just take whatever you want, and I'll take whatever is left and start over." Others take a completely different approach, placing every little thing on the list, all the way down to the DVD player and the food in the pantry, and then systematically go through and divide everything equally. Still, others will list everything and focus on fairness: we both get one good car, one good appliance, one good bedroom set, etc. and then we divide everything else left in the house by alternating turns picking one of what we want until everything is gone. How you decide upon the division of your marital estate is completely up to you.

There is no right or wrong legal way to do it.

Remember to Ask for Things that Are Easy to Forget!

If you have shared a home with your spouse for any length of time, you will naturally remember to put certain things on the list of the things you might want: the Chippendale living room furniture, the master bedroom set, the cars, and yes, the children. However, there are a number of things that people often forget to consider in their list of demands. Don't forget to ask for the things that are sometimes easy to forget!

For example, don't forget to ask for the following things if you want them from the marital estate:

- Artwork

- Burial plots (and pre-paid funeral packages)

- Collector's items (autographs, stamps, rare coins, etc.)

- Family photographs and movies

- Frequent flier miles

- Investment accounts

- Investment properties

- Outdoor furniture and appliances

- Pets/Animals/Livestock

- Retirement accounts (401k, IRA's, etc.)

- Rewards points (from credit cards, department store clubs, etc.)

- Season tickets to professional sporting events

- Timeshare properties

- Vacation homes

- Mineral Rights

As Long As You're Willing to Fight for It, Put It on the List!

Keep in mind that when you come up with your list of wants, this is just a wish list. Depending upon where your spouse is when presented with the list, you may get everything you want, or you might be in for the fight of your life! In this case, you should also be clear about which items you are willing to fight for until the very end – items that you are simply determined not to leave the marriage without, come what may.

For some, this might be the family dog, because besides being like one of your own children, you know that you will want his company when your partner is gone. The dog might even represent everything that your spouse was not: one who was completely faithful, forgiving, and loved you unconditionally. Therefore, you've just *got* to have Fido. If you want Fido, put him on the list.

For others, this might be the Porsche – the one that your spouse spontaneously fell in love with and bought without consulting you. You might not want it because it is so fast and beautiful; you might just want it because your possession of it might represent the ultimate gut punch to your spouse. If you've just *got* to have the Porsche, put it on the list. While you might not get everything on your list, the mere fact that these things are on your list and you are willing to fight for them at least give you a chance at walking away with them.

Step 3:
Find the Right Lawyer

Wait a Minute: Do I *Really* Need a Divorce Lawyer?

When the reality of having to shell out money to pay for a lawyer sinks in, it is not uncommon for some people to pause and ask themselves, "Do I really need a lawyer for a divorce, or can I just do it myself?" This is a good question, and definitely one worth asking before hiring a lawyer. The answer, however, depends on your situation.

If you and your spouse share an apartment, both of you will move out of, both of you have agreed to take your own things and go your separate ways, and you do not have any children or shared assets, then you can do your own divorce! However, as soon as a child and/or substantial assets enters into the equation, things become more complex and you should probably seek out a lawyer.

There are various resources available to help you do your own divorce online, and you can even find "divorce forms" at your local office supply store. Even the state of Texas has developed its own set of forms for people to use when filing for divorce during these tough economic times in which hiring a lawyer can be out of the budget. However, these forms are so generic that if you have any level of complexity involved in your situation, it's hard to get things right. In fact, I have had several clients that have come to me after trying to do things themselves unsuccessfully. In trying to do it on their own, they not only wasted precious time, but they wasted money that they could have used towards hiring professional help.

Generic do-it-yourself divorce forms tend to be in a question and answer type format, and if you do not answer the questions properly, the judge could reject them. Sure, the judge could tell you what to do with your form after seeing that it is wrong, but judges are prohibited from practicing law – and telling you what to do with your forms can be considered "practicing law".

When a judge rejects a person's forms without offering any direction or guidance on how it *should* be submitted, people tend to think that he or she is simply refusing to be helpful; however, they are only following the rules set forth for judges. If you can find any possible way to afford it, even if you have to save up your monies for a little while, hire a lawyer and leave the legal work up to the legal experts!

I Don't Know Any Lawyers! Where Should I Begin?

Now that you've carefully thought through and developed your list of demands, you are armed with what you need to move forward with the next step: finding a lawyer (also known as an *attorney*). A *lawyer* is a legal professional that is authorized to represent you and your interests in a court of law. At the most basic level, a lawyer is just a tool that you use to get what you want; in this circumstance, you want a divorce, and you want to walk away from the relationship with the property included on your list.

People find attorneys in various ways: referrals from friends, family members, co-workers and church members, internet searches, community magazines, they see an attorney's office on their daily drive to and from work, or they might even see or hear a commercial on television or radio.

Regardless of how you find a lawyer, be sure to do some background research on him or her before making first contact. If you received the referral from a person you know, ask about how the attorney is in general as a person. In what types of activities does he or she volunteer? Do people like the person in general? Gather as much information as you can from other people about who the lawyer is when he or she is not in the office.

Then, conduct an internet search.

When doing your online research, search for the lawyer's name. Ask the following questions:

- Does the lawyer have a website? If yes, what information is listed on the website?

- Does the lawyer offer any personal information on the website like hobbies, affiliations, or the name of the church he/she attends (if morality or spirituality is important to you) or does the lawyer keep things all business?

- Is the lawyer local or located in another city?

- Is the lawyer listed in any professional directories?

- Are there photos of the lawyer? Does the lawyer look friendly?

- Does the lawyer look like he/she is no-nonsense?

- How good or poor are the reviews on the lawyer? Do people generally complain that the lawyer is not timely, not a good listener, does not communicate often enough, or is consistently unprepared in court?

- Are there any negative articles or malpractice suits pending on the lawyer?

- Is there a complete absence of information online about the lawyer?

Use all of this information to help you determine whether or not this might be a lawyer that you would want to represent you in court.

A Word to the Wise...

I would <u>caution</u> against using your friend as an attorney – that is, if you still want to be friends when all is said and done! Time and time again, I have seen people hire their friends who are attorneys to represent them in a legal matter, and much of the time, things take a turn for the worse. One reason for this is that friends tend to look for the "friend discount" or the "friend layaway plan" not recognizing that this is what their lawyer-friend does for a living to take care of a family! If the lawyer-friend is not being paid by the client, not only is the lawyer's well-being compromised, but the quality of what the lawyer can offer to other clients is compromised. While the other clients are paying, the lawyer has to take away time from their cases to work on the friend's case who is not paying or paying at a highly discounted rate. Then, rather than the friend having a lawyer that is working with and listening to him or her, they have someone who is resentful and tolerating him or her. Therefore, just because you have a friend who is a lawyer, this does not necessarily mean that this lawyer-friend is the best choice for you!

There are times when using a friend who is an attorney works, because he or she knows you well, already understands your circumstances, and takes a personal interest in seeing you victorious. My advice here, however, is that if you value the friendship and the expertise that your friend has to offer, then offer to pay them their standard hourly rate. In doing so, you demonstrate your level of respect for their practice and your value for the friendship.

Finding Just the Right Match between Your Goals and Your Lawyer's Personality

The most important thing to keep in mind when seeking out a lawyer is that there must be a good fit between you and your lawyer. Just like you seek out a good fit when purchasing shoes, clothes, or even golf clubs, you should do your research to find a lawyer that is a good fit with your personality.

No two lawyers are alike. Each one has a unique way of operating, a personal set of morals, values, and beliefs that drives how cases are handled, varying levels of aggression, and limits to what he or she is and is not willing to do to win a case. When looking for a lawyer who will be a good fit with you, please keep this in mind: "To thine own self, be true". Know what you want and what you do not want in someone who will represent you through this time of crisis in your life, and stay true to these desires in your process of selecting a lawyer. For example, if morality and spirituality are important to you in a lawyer, don't stop until you find someone whose values are in line with your own. Most of all, remain prayerful. Remember: if you are in right relationship with God, you will be able to hear His voice of guidance in selecting a lawyer that is just the right match for you!

If, due to the circumstances surrounding the reason for your divorce, you are feeling especially bitter and resentful, you might be seeking revenge, and undoubtedly, you will absolutely want your partner to pay. In light of this, you are looking for the type of lawyer that most people consider a "pitbull": someone who is super-aggressive and who will go for your spouse's jugular without showing any mercy. It is no accident that lawyers in general have a reputation for being cruel, heartless, and bloodthirsty. There are actually a lot of lawyers like this!

However, for every lawyer that operates with a cutthroat mentality, there are more moderate and even-keeled lawyers who have limits on what they are willing to do to win a case. They operate out of a greater sense of compassion and fairness. Because they have a job to do, they are aggressive concerning the law, but they also have a heart, so they will not destroy someone else just for the sake of doing it. This is the type of lawyer that I am in private practice, and even as a judge, this is the type of character I operate out of today. I wouldn't start the fight, but if you brought the fight to me, I would fight back.

Here's an example. Some people who go through divorce do so with such anger that they are determined to use their children as pawns. They know how much their spouse loves the children and would do anything in the world for the children. Understanding this, they use the children to not only get what they want out of the divorce from their spouse but to just plain get back at their spouse for putting them in this situation.

Therefore, lawyers might get people in their offices that say, "I don't want my spouse to have anything to do with my children!" Some lawyers will reply, "No problem! We can make that happen and we will make your spouse pay!" Other lawyers, however, will ask, "Are you sure that you don't want to remove the children from this adult situation and work through it with your spouse for the children's well-being?" If the client refuses to do so, many attorneys will not take the case.

Some lawyers recognize that when people are dealing with such emotionally volatile situations, they might not be thinking as clearly as they would if they were not in the same situation. Thus, lawyers like me try to talk some reason into their clients, especially when children are involved. All children have a right to have both of their parents in their lives, regardless of how poorly the parents have misbehaved with each other or as individuals. All parents also have a right to have some level of visitation with their children, regardless of the poor quality of decisions they have made.

Even parents who have abused their children have the right to visitation. It is the court's job to ensure that children are protected from an abusive parent, not to keep the parent and child separated indefinitely. In fact, in Texas, the legal code says that the court must try to formulate a visitation schedule for every parent – even abusive ones. These visitations might be less frequent or even supervised, but the goal is not to keep the parent and child apart. Good lawyers understand that children are very forgiving, and they love and need both of their parents in their lives at some level. Therefore, lawyers like this will fight for you while always keeping the best interests of the children in mind.

Every lawyer has a distinct personality. While you are seeking out the one who will represent you in your divorce, make sure that the lawyer's personality matches what you are trying to accomplish. If you want a lawyer who is aggressive and on the offense all of the time, you have every right to seek out someone like this; however, make sure that your final selection is not someone who tends to be the type of person who always strives for peace, pursues fairness at any cost, and always looks for a winwin for everyone. This is not the "pit-bull" you want!

Don't Be Afraid to Screen Your Lawyer: Conduct an Interview!

One of the biggest mistakes people make is simply going with the first lawyer that their friends, family members, or work associates recommend for them. Once they get the phone number to the lawyer's office and place a call, they are often so preoccupied with getting the burning question – *How much do you charge to handle a divorce?* – answered that they forego any additional questions. As long as the lawyer seems legitimate, sounds professional on the phone, and is affordable, the job is theirs! Bad move.

While you are seeking to find the right lawyer to represent you, keep in mind that you are paying someone to perform a service for you. You are hiring someone to work for you just like other employers hire people to work for them! Just as no business owner hires a person without an interview first to determine whether there is a good match, you should not hire a lawyer without first doing an interview to see if there is a good match.

It is not exactly an acceptable practice to go into a lawyer's office and ask, "What's your personality? I need to know so that I can decide whether or not it matches what I need you to do." Instead, there are various interview questions you can ask lawyers that will give you cues and clues to their personality, their philosophy, and their practices.

Additionally, while you are asking your interview questions, take note of how patient the lawyer is throughout the process. If you have 15 questions, does the lawyer patiently take the time to answer each one thoroughly? This might be a patient lawyer. Does the lawyer seem to be getting frustrated after the first eight questions? This might be an impatient lawyer. Did the lawyer, who is a senior partner, see your list of questions on the table and immediately introduce you to a junior associate? This lawyer is probably not interested in working with you on the case. Turn your senses up and take note of every cue and signal you see during the interview process!

Be sure to make a list of *all* of the questions that you desire to ask! When you are in the intimidating environment of a lawyer's office, it's easy to forget things. Consider adding the following interview questions to your list:

- *What is your philosophy on returning phone calls?* This might seem like a simple, unnecessary question, but when you are panic-stricken about some recent development in your divorce, you are going to want a call back! Does the lawyer promise to return your call by the end of the business day? Before leaving the office, no matter what time of the evening that is? By 10 AM the next morning? Within 24 hours? The length of time that you are willing to wait for a call back from your lawyer could be a big factor in whether you choose this lawyer or not.

- *What is your philosophy on responding to e-mails?*

- In the current age of smart phones and immediate access to e-mail, when the vast majority of people are peering down at their smart phones nearly 16 hours a day, some clients demand immediate responses to their e-mail communication. This is not unusual in today's society, which demands instant gratification.

- If you are this type of person, this is an important question to ask during an interview with a potential lawyer. How quickly do you respond to e-mails? When you see my e-mail pop up, are you going to stop and e-mail me back, or do you wait until the end of the business day to return all of your emails? Do you have a 24-hour or one full business day reply policy?

- Depending on how comfortable you feel with the lawyer's response, this might play a key role in your hiring decision.

- *Can I call you on your mobile phone?*

- The lawyer's response to this question will give you an idea about his or her level of accessibility. Some will gladly give you their mobile phone number and welcome you to call whenever you have a question, and they will answer as long as they are not in a meeting or in court. Others will absolutely not give you their mobile number, as they make greater efforts to maintain boundaries between their personal and professional lives. They tend to see the lawyer-client relationship as a strictly contractual agreement that operates during normal business hours like any other company. Allowing you access to their private mobile number would mean that you could access them in the evenings and on weekends, and many find this to be unfair to their own families.

Another reason that some lawyers will not allow their clients to have their personal mobile number is that when people are given such access, they have a tendency to text information and questions – often lengthy ones – and expect an immediate response regardless of the day or time. If the freedom to be communicate in such a manner is important to you, find an attorney that will allow you this level of access.

A Word to the Wise…

While there are several important questions to ask when interviewing a lawyer, there is one that should not be asked: "What is your win-loss record?" Because of the give-and-take nature of divorce negotiations, it is difficult to determine a definite winner and loser. Both parties typically end up with at least *some* of the outcomes they desire, and as a result, both sides are prone to see the same case as a win – or a loss.

- *How much will you charge me for your services?*

Most lawyers will handle a divorce based upon a *retainer agreement*, which is a contract specifying what services they will perform for you and how much these services will cost. Whether they charge one flat fee or charge by the hour, the full amount of what they will charge to handle your divorce should be clearly specified in the retainer agreement or contract.

Keep in mind that attorneys do not just charge for filing papers with the court and standing to represent you before the judge; there are often other expenses associated with the case that should be specified in the retainer. For example, they customarily charge for depositions, civil processing fees, copies, fax transmissions, telephone, and court reporter fees, to name a few.

One of the expenses you should be sure to ask about is that of phone calls. Do they charge you when you make a telephone call to ask them a question? If they do, this is a sign that they probably do not want you to call them repeatedly. If this poses a problem for you, or places you outside of your comfort zone, you might want to consider another attorney.

A *retainer fee* is an advance payment made to the lawyer to perform work on your case. Many lawyers do not require payment for the full retainer up front. For example, while a contract might state that the retainer amount is $5,000 based on the anticipated cost of the divorce, the initial deposit charged might only be $1,500, and the lawyer will allow you to make payments on the balance. Other firms, however, will specify an initial retainer based upon a standard number of hours at the lawyer's hourly rate, the staff's hourly rate, and preliminary expenses. Once this fee is paid, the lawyer will work off of this fee and send you a bill or invoice as the paid fee begins to dwindle. Once the initial retainer you have paid is completely used up, the lawyer will require an additional retainer for the payment of the outstanding balance, if there is one. The lawyer might also request a different amount based upon the complexity of the case and what stage the case has progressed to at that point.

Choose the best lawyer that you are confident that your money will be able to afford, considering your *projected* financial situation over the next several months. The last thing that you would want to happen is to be in the middle of a divorce and realize that you no longer have the ability to pay your lawyer because you had to move into your own place, pay your own bills, pay temporary child support, or temporary spousal support. This would be the equivalent to laying a foundation but not being able to afford to build the house! Being in such a situation could mean the difference between getting what you want and walking away nearly empty-handed. Therefore, do not start building a house that you cannot afford. Think and plan ahead!

- *What forms of payment do you accept?*

This is an important question, especially if you will be paying with a credit card instead of cash. Do not assume that every attorney will have the ability to accept credit cards. Ask! You should also ask if there are any additional convenience fees that go along with paying via credit card and whether your fees can be paid online. If you anticipate making payments via check, find out what the lawyer's check policy is. Do they accept personal checks, or do all checks have to be in the form of certified funds?

- *How will you bill me for your services?*

Different lawyers bill their clients for retainer fees in different ways. Some ask for the full amount of the retainer up front. Some might let you pay half of the retainer up front and pay the rest of the retainer fees in installments as you go along in the process. Some will let you pay an initial retainer fee, and after they have worked a certain number of hours to use up the fees, they will send you an e-mail asking you to pay another retainer fee in order to work more hours on your case. Still others will not require a retainer; they will just bill you for what they need in order to do the work, and after you pay for the hours, they get the work done. However your lawyer bills, make sure that it is clearly stated in your contract, that you know what to expect up front, and that you are comfortable with the billing method.

- *What is your trial strategy?*

This is a more advanced question that most lawyers are never asked, so it signals to a prospective lawyer that you are serious! In asking them how they prepare for trial and what strategy they use, you are instantly putting them on notice that you are an informed client that has done a little bit of homework. I can attest to the fact that when lawyers sense this, they step things up a few notches and pull out their A-Game! They know that in order to keep you with their firm, they are going to have to satisfy you at a different level!

A *trial strategy* is a lawyer's road map for how the case will be handled, starting with the preparation of the petition and going all the way through to the trial and its anticipated outcomes. Once the end is established, the lawyer can work backwards towards the beginning, putting benchmarks down along the way for what needs to be done and by what time. For all intents and purposes, the trial strategy lets you know where you want to be at the end of the trial in order to prepare the case sufficiently.

- *What is your philosophy on necessary vs. unnecessary proceedings?*

When you pose this question to the lawyer, you are asking about stringing things out just because it can be done. Attorneys are notorious for adding fuel to the fire to keep it blazing so that they can keep going back to court and billing you for those hours. Just because it is legal to go to court and file motion after motion does not mean that you should do so. You should want for your attorney to only do what it necessary to get your bottom line goal accomplished. I always say to my clients, "Don't put my children through college when you can put your own children through college." In other words, don't spend all of your money on legal fees when you can be spending it on your own family.

In a lot of cases, it will be up to you to regulate the spending of your hardearned money when working with an attorney. You will have to weigh what you are fighting for with how much it costs to fight and then give your attorney directions on how to proceed. For example, if you are fighting your spouse for a television that cost $1,000 and it takes 10 hours of your lawyer's time to fight for it – at $200 an hour – is it really worth it? Even if you were awarded the television, did you *really* win? The reality is that such a fight was entirely unnecessary. Listen closely to how the lawyer responds to this question about necessary vs. unnecessary proceedings, and then hold him or her closely accountable to it during the legal process.

- *Who will be responsible for producing and paying for trial supplies?*

If you go to trial, there is a strong chance that you will need trial supplies, including exhibits, photographs, audio or video tapes, DVD's, etc. In asking this question, you are inquiring about whether your lawyer will provide the materials or whether you will be required to provide them. Most importantly, you will need to know the cost of these trial supplies are your responsibility and will be included in your invoice.

Usually, gathering trial supplies is done as a joint effort. For example, you might be asked to gather pictures, and then the lawyer's office will arrange and secure them to a presentation board to present in the courtroom. The lawyer might also direct you to a specialist to help you pull voice recordings off of your phone or to assist with other technological tasks so that they can be forwarded to the legal team for preparation. In any case, ask the lawyer to communicate with you up front about who will gather the supplies and how much and when you will be expected to pay for these services.

A Word to the Wise...

If it so happens that, as a result of your extensive list of questions, you get referred by a senior associate (higher level) to a junior associate (lower level). Try to make things work with the junior associate. The junior associate is often more than capable of handling your divorce case and might also charge you a much lower hourly rate! Toss out the notion that tells you that if you are not paying big bucks, you are not getting a good attorney. I always say, "If you can manage a case with an economy car, you don't have to buy a Luxury Vehicle!"

What if I Choose to Represent Myself?

If you choose to represent and speak for yourself in court rather than hiring a lawyer, you are called a *Pro Se*, which literally means "for oneself". The choice to represent yourself in a divorce process is completely up to you. Some people do well representing themselves and others do not – especially concerning operating in a court of law. Court is all about the presentation of evidence. You must be skillful about getting things admitted in front of the judge in order for the judge to actually see it and consider it when making a decision for the final judgment.

There are lots of rules of evidence – legal standards and technicalities – that you must follow in order to have things admitted as evidence in court. If you are not fully aware of all of them, you run the risk that the very evidence that you were sure would make your case or argument a home run could be completely disregarded by the court! Technically, documents that are not presented properly to the court according to the rules of evidence cannot be admitted or considered by the judge in his or her final decision.

Thus, choosing to represent yourself can be pretty risky!

Different judges operate differently under these circumstances; it all depends upon the judge's personality. Some judges will take the attitude, "So you want to do this yourself? Okay! I'm going to treat you just like any other lawyer and hold you to every point of the law. You must do things exactly as a lawyer would, and if you don't, I won't allow your evidence to be admitted!" The attorney on the other side loves judges like these.

However, there are more compassionate judges that take the attitude, "I can tell you need some help here, so I'm going to be more lenient on you. No, you aren't saying things the way they are supposed to be said, but I'll interpret it for you. No, I know that you skipped that critical step when you were trying to present that evidence, but I will allow it to be admitted." The lawyer on the other side has a strong dislike for the practices of judges like these.

A judge can do whatever he or she wants in the courtroom, within the legal limits of the law, of course, when dealing with a Pro Se. This is called *trial court discretion*. Using this discretion, a judge can choose to be as hard or as lenient on a Pro Se as desired, and unless they abuse this discretion, their decisions will be upheld. However, when you make the decision to represent yourself, you do not know what type of judge you will be standing before on the day of your trial. Again, you are taking a big risk when you choose to go the Pro Se route, but the choice is up to you!

A Word to the Wise...

People who neither want to spend what it takes to hire a good lawyer nor want to represent themselves tend to go with a discount attorney – the ones that advertise "Get a Divorce for Only $99!" Beware of these. The only way that a divorce will be $99 is if you have nothing – no money, no assets, no retirement, no children – worth fighting for in a divorce. If you do have anything to fight for, this price is often added on to the base $99 price, and as these extra add-on expenses keep adding up, you can eventually end up paying big money! You could have used this same money to pay a respectable retainer to an attorney that would have given you more personalized attention and quality service.

Keep in mind that since these discount lawyers are only charging $99, they must handle a high volume of cases in order for their business to be profitable. While a standard attorney working on retainer might handle 10 cases over six months, discount lawyers might handle 10 clients a week! This means that you do not receive the attention, communication, and quality that you would receive with an attorney who charges a higher upfront fee.

Step 4:
Determine Your List of Needs

Now that you have decided upon what you want and have identified an attorney that is going to help you get what you want, it is time to identify your needs. Before the lawyer ever files the petition for divorce with the court, you must be able to define what you need, because this information needs to be included with the petition. Once you define your needs, your lawyer will explain to you how the law will respond to your unique circumstances. During the period of time between the filing of the petition and the actual trial, the law will provide for your needs, but only if they are clearly defined. There is no standard list of needs in a divorce; they will differ from situation to situation and from person to person.

Support for Stay-at-Home Parents & Spouses

In Texas, we have temporary spousal support and post-divorce spousal maintenance. These are different than alimony. A judge might order one spouse to pay the other spouse temporary spousal support while a divorce is pending for the purpose of maintaining the family until a divorce is granted and a decree is signed. The support is awarded based on the needs of the spouse needing support and the higher wage-earning spouse's ability to pay.

Post-divorce spousal maintenance is periodic payments from the future income of one spouse for the support of the other spouse. A spouse must qualify for this type of award based on a list of factors, which include but are not limited to the length of the marriage, whether domestic violence was present, the ability of a spouse to provide for him/herself, the level of education of a spouse, whether a spouse has a disability, or whether a child has a disability. Alimony also consists of the periodic payments from one spouse to another as ordered by a decree of divorce, but its qualifications and treatment differ from state to state.

If you are a stay-at-home parent or spouse, your needs will be different from a working parent or spouse. If you are a stay-at-home parent or spouse and have not worked in the last 15 years in order to stay home and raise children, the court might decide that you have no up-to-date, considerable or marketable skills. Thus, in the state of Texas, the court may award you a certain amount of money for a specific amount of time during which you can enhance yourself and develop marketable skills that can help you become self-sufficient. Other states will decide that the stay-at-home parent or spouse is entitled to maintain the same standard of living once you are divorced as you had when you were married. Therefore, they can make the wage earner in the relationship provide monies for you to do so.

Child Support

Child support is money that is ordered to be paid by one spouse to another spouse for the support of a child. Its calculation differs by state. In Texas, it is calculated based on a percentage of the non-custodial parent's earnings. This parent is legally known as the "obligor". The custodial parent who is entitled to receive the child support is legally known as the "obligee".

When making a determination of how much child support must be paid, the court can take into consideration how frequently each parent has possession of the child, but it is not required to do so. The standard guidelines for child support will consider the number of children that are before the court, and, based upon this number, award the custodial parent a certain percentage of the non-custodial parent's earnings. However, in making this determination, the court will also take into consideration whether the non-custodial parent has any other court-ordered child support payments for children that are not a part of the current case. For example, if a husband and wife have three children and the wife is awarded custody of the children in the divorce, the court will grant a percentage of the husband's earnings to the wife as child support based upon these three children. However, if the husband already had three children prior to marrying his current wife, and he has already been ordered to pay child support to his ex-wife, the court will consider these payments when calculating how much child support he must pay as child support to his current wife.

Although there are standard guidelines and traditional percentages that the courts use to determine how much a custodial parent will receive in child support, a court can also choose to award greater levels of child support in amounts that exceed the standard guidelines. This is only done, however, in cases in which certain qualifications are met to justify the court not following the traditional percentages for child support. Typically, these higher awards are based on any special needs of the child and/or the limited financial abilities of the non-paying spouse.

For example, if you have a child with a disability, your child's needs will be different from those of children without disabilities. As a result, the needs of your child will exceed the standard guidelines for child support. However, receiving a child support award that exceeds the standard percentages is not something that is done automatically if you or your child has special needs. You will need to clearly present such matters to the court so that the additional support can be awarded to you.

While in some states, both parents' income is used to determine child support, in Texas, only one parent's income – that of the non-custodial parent – is used to determine child support. If you are the non-custodial parent, even if you earn less than the custodial parent, you will still have to pay child support.

Step 5:
File a Petition for Divorce

What is a Petition for Divorce?

Now it's time to formally set the legal wheels in motion and file a petition for divorce. The petition for divorce is an official request to the court to dissolve your marriage. If you are the one that files for divorce from your spouse, you will be called the *petitioner*, and your spouse will be called the *respondent*. If your spouse filed for divorce against you, your spouse is the petitioner and you are the respondent.

Do I Go to Court Right after the Petition is Filed?

Once your lawyer files the petition for divorce with the court, including all of your wants and needs, what happens next depends on the state in which you live. In Texas, you will have to wait 60 days after the filing of your divorce petition before you can go to court and be granted a divorce. This 60 days is essentially a "cooling off" period; the state, which strongly promotes family, desires to keep families intact. The belief is that if you are angry enough to file for divorce, once you have a month or two to step back from the problem long enough to work through it and cool down, you might reconcile and keep the family together. States have a vested interest in keeping families together and whole!

I have seen the 60-day waiting period work first-hand. The husband filed for divorce; he was very angry. The wife was responsive, but she did not provoke his anger; she was very still about the whole thing and simply said, "Whatever you want." They both had their own lawyers. Sixty-one days after the petition was filed, they showed up at the courthouse ready for their appearance in court.

On the way inside, standing there on the courthouse steps, she had a question for her husband.

"Are you still angry?" she asked.

"No," he replied.

"Do you still want to do this?" she asked.

"No," he again replied.

"Then, why are we here?" she asked, curious.

"Because I didn't think I could stop the divorce once we started it," he explained.

"I never said that," she said, gazing at her husband lovingly. "I'm still willing if you're willing."

With that, they told their lawyers that the divorce was off, and they left the courthouse together. In some cases, 60 days really does work!

Not every state has a 60-day cooling off period; policies vary according to which state you live in, so your lawyer should be well-informed about the state's laws in which he/she practices. For example, in Nevada, under the right set of circumstances, you can be granted an uncontested divorce in as little as two to three weeks. Contrast this with a state like Virginia,

27

which stipulates that under voluntary separation where minor children are involved, you have to live separately for at least one year before an absolute divorce will be granted.

Step 6:
Seek Temporary Orders (If Necessary)

Understanding Temporary Orders

Couples will usually live separate lives while a divorce is pending. However, because they have not formally dissolved their marriage or their life together, there is household business that must be attended to while they wait for their marriage to be officially dissolved. *Temporary orders* are legal rulings by the court that require one or both parties to cease or to do a specific action. They are designed to keep everyone in a balanced place while the divorce is pending until a trial can be held in which the court hears all evidence and makes a final determination.

Your lawyer might seek temporary orders in order to help you maintain the stability of your life, especially when children are involved. For example, your lawyer might seek a temporary order regarding where you or your spouse will live, who gets to live in the house, when and where either spouse will see the children, who will pay the household debts, who will maintain which vehicles and how marital assets will be used while the case is pending, if at all. If only one spouse is working and the other is a stay-athome spouse or parent, the court will issue a temporary order regarding how much the working spouse will pay the stay-at-home spouse or parent and how much the he or she will be allowed to spend while the divorce is pending.

It is not always necessary to have the court's intervention if both spouses can agree to temporary orders. If you are both fairly reasonable and able to negotiate the matter through your attorneys, you can work things out without getting a judge involved. However, if there is a fight over what will and will not be accepted in the proposed temporary orders, you will need to include a third party.

If you will have to involve the legal system to settle your temporary order dispute, you can operate by one of two scenarios. First, your lawyer might recommend that you go to mediation. Mediation is a process in which you use a neutral third party to help you settle your issues rather than going to court. Any decisions reached during the mediation process are legally binding between both parties. (For a more detailed description of the mediation process, see Step 8: Go to Mediation).

If you cannot come to a consensus with your spouse about the terms of your temporary order in mediation, you can take the next step: go to court and let the judge decide. However, keep in mind that the first question that the judge might ask your lawyer is whether or not you have tried mediation first. Lawyers who are familiar with their practice regions will usually know which judges require mediation. If they are unfamiliar with what is required, a call to the court clerks will usually suffice in getting the answer. If you have already gone to mediation on your own, you are one step ahead of things in courts that require the same. If you have not tried mediation before trying to have your case heard in court, the judges who prefer mediation will likely direct your lawyers to try mediation first and to come back only if mediation does not work. Therefore, do not skip this important step when it is known that mediation is a preference or rule in your court.

Going to court for a temporary order can be a pretty serious matter, and this extra trip to court will undoubtedly cost you more time and money as you battle through the process. Hearings for temporary orders are like "mini trials". During a temporary orders hearing, your attorney and your spouse's attorney present evidence that will attempt to persuade the judge to decide in your favor. After hearing all of the evidence, the judge will make the ruling for the temporary order, and both parties must abide by the terms of the order. Violations of the order are considered contempt of court and are punishable by law!

Temporary Orders for Child Custody

When you decide to divorce your spouse, if you have children, they will likely be the first and foremost concern. Both of you will want to know, "Who gets custody?" If one parent desires to have custody and the other does not, the decision is easy. The parents can get an agreed temporary order, or they might even choose to completely forego getting a temporary order; after all, a temporary order is not needed, because the conditions are settled and all child-related issues have been agreed upon.

However, if you and your partner disagree over who should get the children, you will need to obtain a temporary order for child custody and support. When you are seeking a temporary order for custody of the children (also known as seeking to become the *custodial parent*), your lawyer will either seek out a mediator and/or a hearing during which he/she can make your case for custody. To do so, your lawyer will present evidence that you are a better parent than your spouse and that you are more qualified to be the primary caregiver. Your lawyer might also present evidence about why you should be allowed to stay in the house versus your spouse staying in the house. This becomes an especially relevant issue if you are granted custody of the children.

Temporary Orders for Primary Residence

Judges will usually grant a temporary order for possession of the house (the primary residence) to whoever is chosen to be the custodial parent so as to not interrupt the normal routines of the children; just because the parents no longer get along does not mean that the children's lives should be completely disrupted. Thus, the judge will seek to keep the children's daily lives as close to normal as possible by keeping them in the same house, at the same school, in the company of their same friends, and with accessibility to the same activities.

If you have no children living in the home and are battling with your spouse about who will get to stay in the house, if one spouse is better able to afford the house than the other, the court might issue a temporary order for the spouse that can afford the house to stay in it. The other spouse could be ordered to leave the house and find somewhere else to live. The rationale behind this a good one: the court would not want a spouse that cannot afford the house to stay in the house because he or she could potentially lose it. Considering how significant a home is to the couple's shared marital estate – the estate that is up for division – the judge does not want to take this chance. The court also has the option to require the higher wageearning spouse to pay the rent or house note and leave the house while the lower wage-earning spouse remains in the residence. Many scenarios can arise that will affect the outcome of these types of decisions.

When establishing which spouse will stay in the house and which will be forced to find another residence, the court will typically ask for the presentation of several pieces of information including the following:

- Two years of tax returns

- Three recent check stubs

- A list of debts

- A list of monies that are readily accessible

Using these documents, the court will issue a temporary order regarding who will be permitted to reside in the home until the final trial.

Temporary Orders for Other Shared Property & Assets
Oftentimes, a couple will have shared marital assets that are at risk when the relationship goes downhill. Often, the first things either spouse will go after once they realize that the divorce battle is on is the money – transferring monies and clearing bank accounts. In cases like these, in order to protect the monies and assets until it is decided who will receive the funds and how much of them each party will receive, your lawyer might go to court and request a temporary restraining order or injunction to freeze savings accounts, retirement accounts and other types of investment accounts so that neither of you can get your hands on them.

Temporary restraining orders are often issued without notice to the other party. These restraining orders only last for a limited period of time and are designed to give both parties an opportunity to come to court and present their evidence to the judge explaining why they are requesting that temporary orders be issued while the divorce is pending. Once the other party has received notice of what the requesting party is asking for and has an opportunity to prepare for the hearing, the two parties go to court. In court, the person that presented the request for the temporary order can ask for a temporary injunction and for orders that will stay in effect until the divorce is final or until the order is modified due to a change in either party's circumstances while the divorce is pending.

In Texas, temporary restraining orders only last 14 days unless they are extended by the court. They are primarily issued to protect the health and welfare of the parties, their children, and the estate. Receiving a temporary restraining order doesn't necessarily mean that the either party committed any of the acts that the restraining order instructs the parties to refrain from or stop. Instead, being "restrained" by a temporary restraining order just means that if you are engaging in behaviors that can compromise either of the two parties, their children or the property, you should stop. If you are not already doing anything that the temporary order restrains you from doing, don't start.

A temporary injunction is granted after the presentation of evidence, unless terms are agreed upon by both parties without the necessity of a hearing. The injunction usually enjoins parties from engaging in the same behaviors as those outlined by the temporary restraining order; however, the temporary injunction does not expire until a divorce decree is signed or until it is modified by the court.

How Do Temporary Orders Differ from Final Orders?

A temporary hearing issues temporary orders – orders that are only enforceable until permanent decisions are made in the final hearing. The final trial is normally only held after all discovery is completed (see Step 7: The Discovery Period) and the lawyers have had time to build their case, unless an agreement is reached before trial. In courts where mediation is required prior to a final contested trial, the lawyers present their cases before a mediator. This is usually a more preferable way to resolve a divorce, as the two spouses can spend more time and utilize greater creativity when working to arrive at resolutions that work for them. If mediation does not work (or is not attempted), the parties will present their evidence at trial before a judge or jury, and a final order will be issued by the court.

The terms of the final order override any terms outlined in the temporary order, and the outcomes of these two orders might differ. For example, if you had a temporary orders hearing and gained full custody of the children, this might change at the final hearing. Another example is when a temporary order is issued to keep both parties from the unnecessary spending of their shared monies, as this would be considered wasting or misusing community assets. The temporary orders might keep them from making large purchases or from tying up their estate's resources, but the spending freeze would only be temporary.

Lawyers can present all of the same evidence at the final hearing that they presented at the temporary hearing if nothing has changed. However, since the final hearing comes after the discovery period, lawyers might also present new evidence that was uncovered during discovery at the final hearing. Sometimes, lawyers will even have evidence that they *choose not* to present at the temporary hearing; they are saving it for the final hearing in order to strengthen their case. Additionally, lawyers might present new evidence about events and activities that have occurred between the time of the temporary order and the final trial that are likely to affect the judge's decision.

In any case, whatever the judge decides in the final hearing is enforceable by law. Therefore, be careful about what you agree to in an order, and think carefully about how much weight these orders carry before consenting to abide by them. Violating the terms of the final order could be a criminal offense that can be punishable by jail!

Step 7:
Begin the Discovery Period

What is a Discovery Period?

After your lawyer files your petition, the *discovery period* begins. The *discovery period* is a time period during which lawyers investigate who owns what assets and determine which of these assets are considered separate versus those that are considered community property. Those that are considered community property are divisible as part of the marital estate. In other words, your lawyer will try to find out everything that your spouse owns – things that you might not already know about – and your spouse's lawyer will try to dig up the same information about you so that they can determine how that which can be divided should be divided up between you.

During the discovery period, a good lawyer will find out or "discover" a number of things that will provide a good snapshot of everything that will be considered a part of the marital estate, including:

- Locations of your spouse's various bank accounts (both known to you and unknown)

- The value of your spouse's retirement accounts and what type of accounts they are

- What types of fringe benefits your spouse gets at work (car allowance or an actual car, bonuses, stock options, stocks, or travel budgets including per diems.)

- Whether there are any 529 college savings plans for children in your spouse's name

- Any other type of minor accounts

- Property your spouse might have gotten as a gift, inheritance, or owned before marriage.

- How much your spouse makes in gross income (from all sources)

- How much your cars are worth and what you owe on them

- How much your house is worth and how much is owed on it

- Which bills your household has and when they are due

- How much debt you and your spouse have individually and as a couple

You would be surprised to know how little some married couples know about one another, especially as it pertains to finances and assets. While some couples share all of their monies in one account and keep nothing of their own on the side (at least, nothing that their partner knows about), other couples maintain a joint bank account for household expenses and also maintain their own separate accounts with balances that are unknown to their partners. Then, there are also couples who keep everything completely separate and choose to take care of their designated household expenses out of their own accounts. When this happens, their financial information is likely to be unknown to their partner. Since these finances need to be taken into account for the divorce settlement, it is up to the lawyers to uncover not only the monies and assets that are known, but also the ones that the other spouse might be hiding.

Why Does Discovery Seek to Establish Whose "Fault" the Divorce Is?
The laws dictating what can and cannot be legally divided up between you and your spouse when you divorce vary from state to state. For example, Texas is *a no-fault* state. This means that when you file for divorce, you do not have to allege a reason for why you are getting a divorce that puts blame on your spouse. You are allowed to get a divorce by saying, "It's nobody's fault. We just cannot live together anymore because our personalities are different and staying together would be impossible for us."

Establishing *fault,* or blame for the reason behind a divorce is important, because it can have a big impact on your divorce settlement. If you get a nofault divorce and establish that the divorce is, in fact, no one's fault, your marital assets are likely to be divided more equally – 50/50. However, even though you generally ask for a no-fault divorce, you can still specifically request *fault provisions* in the petition. Fault provisions are included in a divorce to establish some level of wrongdoing on either spouse's part, and if these fault provisions are proven in court, it could mean a larger settlement for the party who has been wronged.

For example, fault provisions might include your spouse being cruel to you, abandoning you, or committing adultery. In light of these faults that your spouse committed, you ask the court for more than a 50/50 split of the marital estate; instead, because you have been wronged, you might ask for a 60/40 or a 70/30 split. When you allege that your spouse was at fault and you ask for something other than a 50/50 split in the divorce petition, you are asking for a *disproportionate division* of the marital estate. If you can establish before the court that you have been wronged, by law you might be entitled to it!

No-fault divorces tend to be easier to settle when neither party feels like he or she has been wronged by the other spouse. The parties have simply amicably agreed that they can no longer stay in the marriage because of the high levels of discord existing in the marriage; the conflict of their personalities has marked the legitimate end of their marital relationship, and at this point, there is no reasonable expectation of reconciliation. Plainly put, when a couple seeks a no-fault divorce, they are basically saying, "We don't want to be married anymore, and we are not going to reconcile."

Getting a no-fault divorce, however, does not mean that the divorce will be simple and easy. There are times when neither party is blaming the other for the state of the relationship (it's no one's fault), but they are still fighting over the division of assets, the children, and/or financial support from the other party. In cases like these, even though no one alleges fault, the battle still wages on! In fact, reaching a settlement is oftentimes more difficult to achieve in such cases.

When there is a fault divorce, the circumstances are different. If one party knows that he or she is clearly at fault for the dissolution of the marriage and that because of this, a disproportionate division of the estate is inevitable, this at-fault person is generally more willing to settle the case and move on. In situations like these, both those that are at fault and their lawyers usually know that belaboring the point will not be beneficial to anyone. Instead, dragging things out would only aggravate the already open wound. Seeking a quick closure is usually the best option in these scenarios.

A word to the wise: when people know that they are at fault, their guilt usually makes them more generous in the settlement. However, if the at-fault person is your partner, don't wait too long to settle, because pretty soon, the guilt wears off, the anger sets in, and the battle will be in full force! This tends to happen because the more time goes on, the more they are reminded of the wrong that they have committed; if you combine this with the additional money they are spending in the legal process, they become less apologetic and start becoming more irate. In fact, they might even become vested in the belief that the wrong they committed was only done because of the behavior of their spouse and that they were in fact the victim, not victimizer! Understanding where a person's breaking points are is critical in settlement negotiations where fault is present. For best results, when dealing with an at-fault spouse, close quickly before this breaking point is reached!

There are some states that actually *require* one of the spouses to allege fault or place the blame and responsibility on someone for the destruction of the marriage! If neither party alleges fault, many states have lengthy waiting periods before the divorce can be finalized. If fault is alleged, it still has to be proven, and it may or may not affect the property division or childrelated issues. In Texas, alleging certain faults will allow you to waive the 60-day waiting period to be granted a divorce.

If you allege that your spouse was at fault and wronged you in some way, it is your lawyer's job to get to the bottom of things by launching an investigation into your claims. This investigation occurs during the discovery period. For example, if you claim that your partner committed adultery – had an affair with another person while you were married – your lawyer will try to "discover" when it happened, who it happened with, and how long it went on.

In some of the discovery tools used to determine the existence of a marital affair, an adulterer is legally sworn to tell the truth about the affair. Usually, the spouse accused of having the affair will try to play things down by saying, "It was just dinner! I felt nothing for that person!" They recognize that if the adultery itself can be proven by factual or substantive circumstantial evidence, this could put them at fault and affect their part of the division of property.

Alleging that your partner was at fault is not the only way to be awarded a disproportionate division of the marital estate. You can be awarded a disproportionate division without fault if, for example, your health is failing but your partner's health is fine, if you have a disabled child and it is determined that you will be the one paying for his or her expenses, or any wide range of factors that suggest that you will need *more than* the traditional 50/50 split.

The key to being awarded the disproportionate division of the marital estate in this case is to put your spouse on notice at the beginning of the case so that your spouse can know what he or she is defending. By law, your spouse has to be given an opportunity during the discovery period to ask all questions that are necessary to determine what you do and do not qualify for in terms of the split of the estate and support.

How Is Discovery Conducted?

Typically, your spouse's lawyer will send a written request for discovery to your lawyer, and your lawyer will forward the request to you. Lawyers can perform discovery by gathering information in multiple ways:

- Interrogatories – A list of questions which may be general in nature or specific to your situation. They are usually limited in number.

- Request for Production – A request for parties to produce copies of documents for inspection and copying, which consists of financial documents, documents relating to property, bank statements, mortgage or deed information, and other pertinent documents or statements.

- Deposition – The testimony of a witness taken outside of the courtroom. They are recorded by a stenographer or court reporter, and they are sometimes videotaped.

- Deposition by Written Question – A list of questions submitted usually to a non-party who has information significant to the case. These questions are to be answered under oath.

The discovery period in divorce cases usually lasts until 30 days before the trial, but this time can be altered based on the court or special circumstances of the parties.

Important Things to Know about Answering Questions during Discovery

Whether you are trying to prove that your spouse is at fault or your spouse is trying to prove that you are at fault, keep in mind that you are both expected to tell the truth about it. In fact, you can legally get into trouble if they can prove that you were not telling the truth during discovery. How they choose to respond if they find out that you were not telling the truth will vary. While you might not be brought to trial by the District Attorney for lying, your spouse's lawyer might bring up the fact that you lied to the judge later on in court. This will inevitably affect the judge's perception of you as an honest person and affect your credibility in the eyes of the court. Consequently, this might affect how much you get in the division of property.

Expect for the lawyers questioning you to ask you some very intimate questions about the relationship you allegedly had – very intimate. Don't be shy or intimidated by them; lawyers are accustomed to hearing everything under the sun. Their interest is not for the purpose of getting deeply into your personal business so much as it is hearing your story to build their case.

Always remember that you should never answer questions from another lawyer without your own lawyer present – unless you are representing yourself. The opposing counsel (your spouse's attorney) is not permitted to ask you questions regarding the case without your lawyer present unless your lawyer consents to the questioning, which most lawyers would *never* do under *any* circumstances. Lawyers are very protective of their clients and very untrusting of other lawyers!

Step 8:
Attempt to Work Things Out in Mediation

The Precursor to Your Day in Court: Working Things Out through Mediation

Once your attorney and your partner's attorney have completed their discovery and have all of the information they need, they can build a case and prepare for the trial; however, the case does not necessarily go straight to court. Different courts within different counties operate according to their own local rules and policies, and these policies often include sending the couple to mediation before sending them to a courtroom to stand before the judge.

Mediation, (also known as *alternative dispute resolution*) is an informal way to settle a dispute or controversy using the participation of a trained third party – a *mediator*. Simply put, before sending you into a courtroom to have your dispute settled by a judge or jury, you might first be asked to settle your issues with your spouse using a mediator. In mediation, you and your spouse try to agree on what should happen to everything from the children to all of the assets and liabilities in your marital estate. If you are able to successfully come to a settlement using a mediator, you save the busy and overtaxed courts – and yourself – both time and money.

Mediation Has Its Benefits!

There are sure benefits to being able to settle your divorce dispute in mediation. The main benefit is that you can take your time to arrive at a win-win outcome that is acceptable for both you and your spouse. You see, the court only has so much attention to give your case. Because of the number of cases they have to see on a daily basis, you will never get 100% of the judge's time and attention. Usually, when they make a ruling, they are ruling according to one standard they use across the board rather than giving special consideration to your unique circumstances.

For example, let's say that your spouse works a non-traditional job on a rotating shift and is only available to keep the kids every other week on Tuesdays, Wednesdays, and Fridays from 7 AM to 7 PM, then, Mondays, Tuesdays, and Saturdays from 7 AM to 7 PM on alternate weeks, and a total of 30 days during the summer, only if the days are broken up into increments. This best fits your spouse's schedule, and you are fine with it. You can specify these unique visitation terms among yourselves in mediation. However, if you leave such things up to the judge to decide, he or she might issue a final order that your spouse's visitation is Friday from 6 PM to Sunday at 6 PM every other week on the 1st, 3rd, and 5th weekends with thirty consecutive days in the summer. The judge simply does not have time to pull out a calendar and look at every other week, coordinating things with your schedule!

Again, the judge is using a familiar, across-the-board, standard possession schedule and will not take the trouble to look at your or your spouse's rotating schedule. Courts are programmed to stick as closely as possible to the visitation standard of their state. Their child visitation standards are based upon research about "what works best for the children" versus being based upon what fits best within the schedules of Mom and Dad. Therefore, to ensure that you get the terms you want, do the legwork yourselves in mediation instead of leaving it up to the judge.

Your lawyer might also use mediation to come up with some of the terms that you will ask for in the final hearing. For example, even if you cannot settle *everything* in mediation, you should be able to settle *some* things. You might be able to settle the child visitation schedule amongst yourselves, even though you could not work out win-win terms for the division of the marital estate. In such case, your lawyer would inform the judge that you have agreed upon the child custody and will only need the court to decide the matter concerning who will receive what monies or assets. Once the contested issues are brought before the court, the judge will normally accept your agreement on the settled matters and only hear the contested matters. If, however, the judge does not consider the visitation schedule agreed upon by the parents to be in the best interest of the child, he or she may not accept the visitation schedule that you have put together. In such instances, the judge, operating within his or her trial discretion, will give you another opportunity to work out a better schedule. If you and your spouse cannot do so, the judge will likely reject the proposed schedule and put his or her own schedule in place for the best interest of the child.

Step 9:
Go to Trial and Fight
for What You Want & Need!

Any time you are preparing to go to court, whether you are headed for a temporary hearing or a final hearing, you might be asked to see a mediator first. It is often only after you are unsuccessful at settling your dispute with a mediator that you are allowed to have your case taken to trial and be decided by a judge or jury. A *trial* is an event in which two parties engaged in a dispute come together to present facts, evidence and arguments for examination by a judge or jury.

There are two kinds of trials: civil and criminal. Your divorce trial will be a civil trial. You may opt to have a trial by judge or by jury. In family law, which is the type of law that divorce cases fall under, only some issues can be handled by a jury. Even with the jury's involvement, other issues might still need to be handled by the judge.

What to Expect on Trial Day

Your lawyer will notify you of your trial date in advance so that you can clear your schedule for the entire day. A good lawyer will brief you on what to expect on the day of the trial so that you can understand what is going on and be mentally prepared for it all. Anxiety usually centers on what is unknown; thus, to keep my clients from becoming anxious, I try to answer any questions and eliminate any confusion for them about the day's events.

For example, I prepare my clients for their day in court by discussing the following items:

• *The location of the trial*

It is a good idea to take a day to drive to the courthouse in advance so that you know exactly where you are going. Often, a courthouse is located in a complex of buildings, so in order to avoid confusion and potentially getting lost on the day of your trial by going into the wrong building, scope things out before-hand. If you are the type of person who gets nervous about driving downtown (especially because in some cities there are numerous one-way streets), which is often where the courthouse is located, it is definitely a good idea to drive the route one or two times before the day of your trial.

• *Where to park*

Most of the time, clients will have to drive to the courthouse during rush hour traffic and fight with many others for limited parking spaces. Thus, I encourage them to make note of how to access parking areas when they scope out the trial location, including how much parking will cost if it is a paid lot (so they can bring cash if necessary). Also, I encourage my clients to have a Plan B for where to park, just in case the parking lot or parking garage is full upon their arrival. Identifying these sites is always best done prior to the day of the trial instead of trying to figure things out on the day of the trial. Having a game plan that you have already scoped out will make things more familiar and less stressful for you.

• *Security requirements*

I always inform my clients about how long the security lines will be. I also let them know that they can expect to go through the same security routine that they would go through at an airport. They will have to remove their shoes, belt, change from their pockets, and other metals. They will have to send their purses and phones through the screener. If they walk through the security stand and it beeps, they will be pulled aside by an officer who will ask them to extend their arms and legs, and he or she will screen them with the security wand or ask them to remove whatever item caused the beep. Long lines and hold-ups at security are probably the number one reason that clients panic, especially when they are running late to court. The security line takes time, so prepare in advance by arriving early!

- *Where to meet the lawyer*

Your lawyer should tell you exactly where to meet him or her. It may be in the courtroom, outside of the courtroom, or in some other common area within the courthouse. One of the things that I am always sure to tell my clients is that if you do not see me when you get into the courtroom, do not panic! I am coming! Often, lawyers will be in another courtroom with other clients or wrapping up some other legal matter in the courthouse, but they are aware of your trial time and location, and they will be there, so don't stress. Judges also understand this. If you are in the courtroom and they call your name and docket number without your attorney present, they will simply push your case further down on the docket until your lawyer arrives. Still, remember: don't stress!

- *What to expect inside of the courtroom*

I always tell my clients to expect a lot of people in the courtroom. You will not be sitting in front of the judge with just you, your spouse and your respective attorneys discussing your case in private! Instead, expect a room full of people to be there witnessing the proceedings. There are times when you are the last case to be heard or the only trial scheduled because of a special setting, but these are the exceptions not the norms.

Expect to sit and wait until your case is called on the docket. While you wait, out of respect for the court, take note that you cannot bring newspapers to read. Instead, because court is not that interesting, bring something to read on your tablet or your smart phone. However, ensure that your phone ringer is turned off! Judges are very particular – very serious – about not hearing phones ringing or people talking on them in their courtrooms. If you have to take a call, put your phone on silent so that you can see it if it rings, and then step out to answer it if necessary.

You can also expect to see a jury box, lawyers, a court reporter, and a law enforcement officer (usually in uniform) who is enforcing order in the courtroom. You will also see an area that divides the gallery, where everyone is sitting, and the area where the judge and court personnel are sitting and working. The railing or partition that divides it is called "the bar". Only court personnel lawyers, witnesses and those person granted permission are permitted to pass this area. One of the purposes of the division to be able to keep the orderly conduct of business flowing without interruption and to distinguish the lawyers from the litigants.

- *What to expect during the trial*

At some point, expect for the judge to do a docket call. When you hear your name, your lawyer will stand and make announcements if they are present. If they are not present the court will expect you to respond and let them know if you have a lawyer. If your lawyer will not be present at docket call it is customary for them to notify you and the court of their location and estimated arrival time. When it is time for your case, your lawyer will signal for you to come forward and sit or stand beside him or her for the trial.

During the trial, you can expect your lawyer to present evidence, including photos, documents, sound recordings, etc., and to call and question witnesses from the witness list. As the judge listens to the presentations, he or she may or may not be nice; however, do not take this personally. Take all of your cues from your lawyer and just do what your lawyer says.

Giving Children a Voice in the Trial

You might wonder whether or not your children will have to represent themselves in court because of your decision to go through a divorce. The good news is that they do not. Instead, in divorce cases, an *amicus*, which is a legal representative for your child who speaks to the court on behalf of the child, might be appointed. The job of the amicus is to ensure that the best interests of the child are being represented in the court. In fact, having an amicus is like having a completely different attorney that is appointed just for the children. Of course, this will translate into more money that you will have to spend, because an amicus can be expensive.

It is also possible for a child to have an *ad litem* in court. In Texas, an ad litem is an attorney that can represent a child or an adult in court. In some jurisdictions, having an amicus and an ad litem is interchangeable. However, an amicus is a representative of the court that is an attorney who is appointed to gather information to present to the court that will give light to the issues which impact the child in the case.

There is a way to avoid the expense of having to hire an amicus: work things out with your spouse considering the best interests of your children rather than focusing on your own. No one knows your children like you and your spouse, so no one, not even an amicus, can speak to the court on behalf of your children like you can. Therefore, do all you can to work together for the best interests of your children before this privilege is taken away from you and given to an amicus.

When matters of custody are hotly contested and the parties can afford it, an amicus is appointed. If parents cannot afford an amicus, sometimes there are legal services that will provide them free of charge (pro bono). Parents can contest the appointment of an amicus or argue that the party who is perceived to be the most unreasonable should have to pay all or the majority of the amicus fees.

How Can I Make the Divorce Process as Pain-free as Possible?

Divorce is never easy. However, after decades of working in the legal arena, I have observed and experienced certain practices that make the difference between a good, easy-as-possible divorce and those that turn into long, drawn-out nightmares.

The key to making the legal side of your divorce as pain-free as possible is being an informed client. In order to be an informed client, make sure that you have a full understanding of the steps that I have outlined for what to expect in the divorce process.

Now that you have a list of steps to DO, here are a list of steps to BE that will help to make your divorce as smooth as it can be:

- Be <u>careful</u> to pick the right lawyer

- Be <u>specific</u> in making your lists (of assets, of what you want, of what you want for the children, of what was yours before marriage.)

- Be <u>thorough</u> in gathering all of your support documents

- Be <u>patient</u>, not anxious

This last "Be" (be patient) is a particularly important one that I like to discuss with all of my clients. Divorces don't just happen overnight. They can last anywhere from a couple of months to a couple of years depending on how much is at stake in the marital estate. There might be times when you are simply waiting... and waiting.

Your attorney should keep you posted about important dates and what you should and should not be doing during these seasons of waiting. The key, however, to not driving yourself crazy while you wait is knowing that your attorney is on the job working behind the scenes on things that you do not see. For example the discovery process on your side or your spouse's side could be moving slowly and delay the process.

Even though you are not directly involved, things are happening! Therefore, it is unnecessary to call your attorney repeatedly to ask the same questions over and over again: "Why don't we have a court date yet?" "Why is the courthouse so far away?" "What is taking so long?" The divorce process can be a slow one, but it works. Also, keep in mind that your attorney might be charging you for each of these phone calls, so only call when necessary!

Also, consider that you are not the only client that your lawyer has; divorces could go faster if attorneys only had to deal with one client at a time. There might be a season when your attorney is fully engaged with another client during your waiting period so you might not be getting daily – or weekly – communication. If you feel that you have been patient with your lawyer and just need to be reassured that things are still in progress, pick up the phone and call. If it will give you peace of mind that everything is going according to plan, shoot your lawyer a quick e-mail or use their preferred method of communication and ask for an update. Just like with anything else, it is the squeaky wheel that gets the oil.

The Final Thing to Expect: The Fight of Your *Life*!

In summary, there are several things that you can expect when you are expecting to get a divorce. Expect to spend several days and hours of your time with your lawyer during the process. Expect to have to take off of work to meet with your attorney at his/her office during the day, because many attorneys do not have late evening hours or weekend hours. Expect to have to do some homework like doing research regarding your property and gathering documents, which will take hours after work and on weekends. Expect to go to trial and be there all day without getting frustrated about how long things are taking. Expect to persevere through the process; it is so demanding that often, one spouse will give up the fight and give you whatever you want – if what you want is tangible.

Finally, expect for the next 2 to 18 months to be one of the most trying and challenging seasons you have ever experienced in your life, not only legally, but emotionally. It's time to put your game face on, because it's time to fight. However, as informed as you are about the legalities of divorce, you cannot fight until you can pull yourself together and deal with where you are emotionally. Despair. That is the next step in the journey. Turn the page, and let's take it together.

A Prayer for Direction...

Before moving on to the next chapter, pray this prayer aloud:

Lord, I thank you for revealing to me the knowledge that I will need to legally move forward with a divorce. I pray that you would strengthen me to handle every aspect of it, from choosing the right lawyer, to establishing a strategy, to developing a settlement that is fair and equitable with my spouse. I pray that you would keep my mind settled and at peace as I keep my mind on You throughout this process. Empower my lawyer every step of the way as he/she represents me. Help us to work as a team and operate together in a decent, respectable manner that exemplifies love, justice, and equity and that will glorify You. Thank you that even though the judge makes the ruling, You have the final say. Therefore, Lord, I will trust You to lead me into the legal process, through the legal process, and out of the legal process with a praise on my lips! Amen!

CHAPTER TWO

It's Not "Just You": Mind-Numbing Grief is *Normal* in Loss!

The First Consultation: Why Didn't You Write Anything Down?

Being a divorce attorney can be pretty tricky business. Unlike most other attorneys, divorce attorneys are expected to wear two hats: lawyer *and* psychologist. This is understandable when you consider the state of the typical divorce case client: traumatized, completely grief-stricken, and confused, all at the same time.

While they are trying to fight their legal battle, they are simultaneously trying to come to terms with the end of the most significant relationship in their lives. As such, they are always looking for someone to talk to as a make-shift therapist. Someone who might *possibly* be able to help them understand why they are where they are. Someone to help them answer at least a fraction of the thousands of questions zooming around a mile-aminute in their heads. Someone with whom they can share their mindnumbing grief about the unbelievable, unjust, and "it's just not fair" circumstances that brought them into a lawyer's office. Who better to talk to and help them understand their fate than an attorney that handles divorce cases for a living, right?

If you were coming to my office for your first consultation about your impending divorce today, I could pretty much predict how things would go. First, I would ask you why you were here today. Then, you would begin to tell your story: everything started off really well, and you were very happy until, out of the blue, something unexpected and devastating happened. Next, you would go into an explanation of not knowing how things got to this point in your relationship; you don't know what happened or how you got here. Then, because you are in the midst of what is perhaps the greatest grief of your life, the waterworks would come: uncontrollable tears that you promised you would not cry when you went to see the attorney.

I would pull the tissue box close to you – I have learned to keep an ample supply of them in my office – and I would listen patiently to the details of how your life has been unraveling at the seams before your very eyes as you helplessly try to keep the pieces together. Then, you would make a futile effort to put into words things which cannot be sufficiently expressed with a limited human vocabulary: how much you hurt, how deeply you hurt, how debilitating your hurt is, how your hurt is making it impossible to live a "normal" life, and how living in such a state is new territory for you. You're usually able to shake setbacks off and pull yourself together – the strong person you are – but this is different. It's a body blow that has left you hurt in places you never realized had the capacity to feel pain, dazed to the point that it takes strong effort to think clearly, and confused about life as you know it or as it will be in the future.

Eventually, after you had emptied out your heart, it would be my turn. I would tell you what I tell all of my clients in such a state: I understand where you are. You are normal. Despite how it feels right now, you are going to be okay. You have suffered a severe loss, so what you are going through is a natural and expected part of the grieving process. Finally, I explain to you that the process that you are about to go through to legally dissolve your marriage will take some inner strength and a sound mind, so you *must* deal with this grief and pull yourself together; you will need all of the gumption that you can muster up to deal with *this* battle! Then, you would wipe your tears, nod your head, and watch me pull out my legal pad to get started. It might have taken more than an hour (yes, a billable one!) to get to this point – the point at which we could finally start getting some real legal work done – but at least we got here.

I recall one client who came to me for an initial consultation who went through this very process. At the end, he asked me, "Why didn't I write anything down?" I replied, "You didn't give me anything that I could use!" Overtaken with grief, he'd spent an entire hour in my office talking about his big break-up and the pain associated with it. As heart-wrenching as his story was, I could not sue for any of it. Grief is not admissible in a court of law.

Exactly What *Is* Grief?

While most have experienced various levels of grief at some point in life, few have taken the time to understand the formal definition of it and the research that exists behind it. According to Merriam Webster Dictionary, grief is a noun that is defined as:

Deep sadness caused especially by someone's death; a cause of deep sadness[1]

Grief is caused be the unfortunate, yet inevitable, loss of a loved one. The loss of a spouse can occur in one of two ways: through literal death or through divorce. It is said that divorce is like experiencing the physical death of a spouse – without the support, understanding, or the rituals afforded when one physically dies. Both types of loss ultimately lead to an intense sense of grief.

In divorce, while you do not face the physical loss of your partner to death, you do experience the permanent removal of the person from your life. The time, resources, intimacy, and love you once shared with one another are a thing of the past – just like one would experience with the physical death of a partner. The future that you planned for and dreamed of sharing with this person must now be re-calculated, because your loved one is no longer there – just like one would experience with the physical death of a partner. Thus, even though your partner is still walking the earth, you experience the same level of grief as if he or she had passed on to eternity.

In fact, the grief of divorce can be even more magnified, because we often feel that we should have greater control over such situations. As a result, we personalize the failure that has led to our grief, which adds guilt to the equation. Additionally, if we still desire to be in the relationship, we hold out hope that reconciliation will occur. When it does not, our grief is magnified even greater: the idea of being permanently rejected by someone we desire to be with is anguishing. Each time we see the person that we so desperately love, while being powerless to re-establish the relationship we desire with them, is like experiencing the same loss all over again, day in and day out. So, you see, the grief of divorce can be even greater than that of death.

---

[1] "grief." Merriam-Webster.com. 2014. http://www.merriam-webster.com/dictionary/grief

Kübler-Ross' Five Stages of Loss and Grief

In 1969, Swiss-American psychiatrist Elisabeth Kübler-Ross published a groundbreaking book entitled *On Death and Dying*[II]. In this book, she used years of research developed while working with terminally-ill patients who were dealing first-hand with the process of grief surrounding the inevitable end of their lives and with their families. Through this research on death and dying, Kübler-Ross developed a theory that grief was not a onedimensional emotion, but rather a pattern of adjustment that was comprised of five different stages.

Kübler-Ross' Five Stages of Loss & Grief

- Denial

- Anger

- Bargaining

- Depression

- Acceptance

These five stages of loss and grief are universal; because everyone will at some point experience loss, death of a loved one, and mourning, everyone will experience at least one or more of these stages of grief.

Understanding that grief is not merely an emotion but a process that includes a pattern of adjustment to one's circumstances helps those coping with grief to better understand why they seem to be experiencing so many different thoughts and feelings over the loss of a loved one. The stages make them aware that they can expect to navigate through not just one particular state, but a series of states – or stages – before the process of grief is ultimately resolved. Thus, instead of feeling out of control with their fluctuating, ever-changing emotions, their sense of loss and grief are affirmed as being… normal.

As we go through the process of mourning and bereavement that is called grief, it is important to understand several things about the stages:

[II] Kubler-Ross, E. (1997). On Death and Dying. New York: Simon & Schuster.

- People do not necessarily go through the five stages "in order" (we often move between stages before arriving at acceptance), and this is okay.

- Because people are different, they approach each of the stages differently.

- Different people spend different lengths of time in each stage.

- The way that people express each stage might be more or less intense than others, depending on the person and the stage.

Let's face it: you are grieving. As much as you try, you can neither deny where you are nor ignore where you are. What's more, you cannot suppress the emotions you are feeling, allowing them to linger just under the surface. This lingering will lead to unresolved issues that will eventually affect your mental and physical well-being, relationships, and overall quality of life. Sooner or later, you will explode (or even worse, implode), which will inevitably cause collateral damage to others and the world around you! Instead, each stage of your grief must be dealt with in order to produce a healthier you that is at peace with your situation, the world around you, and yourself.

What are you feeling right now? Denial and isolation? Anger? Making bargains with a Higher Power to get your spouse back? Depression? Or have you ultimately accepted the fact that things are over for good and arrived at a sense of peace about this conclusion? Understanding where you are in the grief process will help you put into context exactly where you are so you can work through the stages properly.

As an attorney, I can tell you from experience that understanding where you are in the stages of grief can really make a difference as you approach the legal process of dissolving your marriage. You must be able to approach the process with a sound, rational mind. This does not mean you cannot begin the legal process of divorce if you are in one stage or another in the process of dealing with your grief. It does mean that as you approach the legal process, you are aware of your mental state and how each of the states can either positively or negatively affect the decisions you will have to make and the approaches you will take.

How Can Grief Impact the Process of Divorce?

In the chapters to come, I will take you through each stage of loss and grief in more detail in order to help you identify where you are so you can keep these things in mind. However, allow me to first give you some insight into why working through your grief is so important. If you do not work through it, it could end up having a significant impact on your divorce and those around you!

There are various ways in which unresolved grief can impact the legal process of divorce.

Impact 1: It Can Make a Divorce Cost as Much as a Luxury Vehicle!

Whether you have filed for divorce or are responding to a partner who has filed for divorce, you should understand that when you hire a lawyer, you are going to have to spend some money. However, as I tell my clients, "Divorce does not have to cost as much as a luxury vehicle!" When your mind is straight, you have a handle on your grief, and you are focused on the ultimate end – dissolving the marriage in a way that is reasonably fair for the both of you – you can keep your costs under control and maximize your money. However, if you are still operating out of your emotions and bogged down by your grief, you can be assured that not getting a handle on things will invariably cost you – significantly! Not having a handle on your grief will make your divorce more difficult, more expensive, and more hurtful than it has to be!

When you approach a lawyer to handle your divorce, you are hiring a legal representative – a professional whose purpose is to help you legally dissolve your marital union in a court of law. You are not hiring a psychologist! When you consider that an attorney can charge $200 - $500 an hour to handle your divorce, would you rather spend your hours using him/her as a shoulder to cry on, or would you rather spend your hours talking about the legal facts? Just in case you're still pondering this, let me help you: talk about the facts.

At the end of the day, if you have to spend, for example, $5,000 on a divorce, you will want to know that you spent your hard-earned money on professional legal services. If you just need a listening ear, call up a couple of friends, ask them to meet you for coffee, and pour your heart out with them – not your attorney. Remember: your friends will listen to you share about your grief for free – or at least for the price of a cup of coffee – but your attorney will listen for $200 - $500 an hour. I think using the listening ears of your friends is a better bargain, don't you?

If you need a professional to listen and help you work through things, use a mental health professional, not a legal professional. You will often find your employer-provided health insurance will cover a certain number of hours of counseling or psychiatric wellness visits, and all you have to do is pay a low co-pay, if anything at all. Again, this is a much better option than spending hundreds of dollars an hour trying to get your lawyer (who is trained in the law, not mental health) to help you work through the process of your grief.

In sum, in order to use your dollars most efficiently when you go through a divorce, keep in mind the following tips:

1. Know where you are in working through the five stages of grief so you can know whether you are mentally ready to engage the services of a legal professional.

2. Use your lawyer as your lawyer, not as a shoulder to cry on or a listening ear.

3. Use your health insurance to pay for visits for a professional counselor, if needed.

4. Only approach a lawyer when you have a handle on your grief – whatever the stage – and are ready to get some *real* legal work done.

5. Approach meetings with your lawyer ready to share facts, not feelings, because facts are what matter most in a court of law.

Impact 2: It Can Make a Divorce Last as Long as a Presidential Campaign!

When you break a divorce down to the fundamental essence of what it is, divorce is really only about deciding how two people can split up what they have and end the relationship. Coming to an agreement on this does not have to last a year and a half or more! In fact, coming to such an agreement depending on the size of the estate, may take only a few weeks – that is, if you and your spouse are both thinking clearly and not operating out of your grief.

Time after time, I have seen either my client or my client's spouse drag things out, all because they are bogged down by the grief of the divorce. This action is not a harmless one: there is a time value of grief. The longer you allow the divorce process to be drug out, the more hurt you will both experience, the longer it will take the children to adjust to the situation, and the longer it will take for you to come to a place of finality so that you can begin to build a new life. These effects are, in and of themselves, losses.

For your own sake, and for the sake of others, once you make the decision to divorce, determine to "just get it done". Once you realize that reuniting or reconciliation are not possible, stop rehashing what should have happened or what could have been. Stop picking at the sores of the past, and allow them to heal. Stop looking back, cut your losses, and move forward. Again, you can "get it done" even while you are in the process of grief; you will just have to be keenly aware of where you are in the five stages and allow your rational focus to drive you rather than your emotions.

I recall a couple that I was working with to develop a cooperative agreement for their divorce. This simply means that they were trying to work together to come up with a plan on how to split up what they had and just end the marriage. As they sat side-by-side in the chairs across from my desk, I could sense the tension that was growing in the husband as the wife, bogged down by grief, continued to drag things out.

The process should have been a relatively simple one: after 30 years of marriage, he filed for divorce, but she did not want the divorce; however, she did not want to fight him because she did not want him to be angry with her, because then, she would surely not be able to get him back. She agreed to come to my office to develop the cooperative agreement, even though she was completely against it. As we worked through the agreement, he would propose something, and then ask her if she was okay with it. She would reply, "Whatever you want to do, but I don't want this divorce" to every single question. Out of his love and compassion for his wife, the husband was trying to be as patient as possible. However, after repeated rounds of this response resulting in not being able to come to any firm conclusions, he finally said, "Enough! I hear you! You don't want the divorce, but I do!"

This process, which should not have been highly complex, requiring only a small number of hours, took twice as long as it should have taken. Therefore, not only did it double the time, it doubled the money they had to pay. Because she did not have a handle on her grief when she came into my office, she was in a passive resistant mode – a mode which always means that things are going to take longer than necessary. My heart went out to her, because I realized that dragging the process out was her way of holding on to her husband for as long as possible. The grief of facing such loss was something that she was just unwilling to confront, so she attempted to avoid the confrontation. She passively fought the resolution all the way by feigning agreement while withholding acceptance. Eventually, we were successful in helping the couple divorce, but not without the additional costs of prolonged hurt, time, and money.

There is another situation that I am reminded of in which a husband did not want to let the relationship go, but the wife was firm on her decision to divorce. She had come into my office and just filed the divorce papers; all he had to do was sign them, and she was going to take care of the legal fees and the court appearance. Thus, this should have been a quick, easy case, right? Wrong.

When the husband came into my office, filled with grief, he was only supposed to be there to sign the decree and tell me when his wife could come pick up her things from their home. However, instead, he kept me hemmed up in my office for over two hours telling me stories about why he was experiencing such hurt, pain, and grief over the loss of his wife. Yes, these hours were billable… to her. Then, to make matters worse, he decided to drag the process out further by making it impossible for her to pick up her personal belongings! He was intentionally uncooperative. At first, he told her that she had to come get her things from the house. Later, he changed his mind; he would not let her come to the house to retrieve her belongings because it would be too painful for him to witness such a final act. He said that he would bring her possessions to her, but he took forever doing it. Eventually, he brought ten boxes of her items to my office, and I had to store them for her until she could come to retrieve her personal effects. Of course, many firms would bill for this kind storage privilege.

During this long, drawn out process, he would also send his wife very long e-mails and then call me to ask if I would call her to tell her to open up her e-mail and read his messages. Then, he would send me a copy of the very long e-mails in hopes that I would communicate what I had read to her! I recognized that all of these actions were the delay tactics of a grieving husband, and my client had no time for such behaviors. After all, time is not only money. Remember, time has a value in and of itself, as well.

The reality of the matter is that in holding my client's possessions hostage, out of his grief, he was trying to hold on to his relationship and stay connected to his wife, whom he loved dearly. He simply was not ready to let go. As long as he had her possessions, she still technically lived at the house and there was no finality to the end of the marriage. He was buying himself some time – some space to argue his case – hoping that at some point, things would change. Eventually, my client retrieved all of her personal items and was granted her divorce. However, again, the process took significantly longer than was necessary given the short length of the marriage and the few possessions they had acquired.

When people are trying to drag out a divorce, lawyers can see it coming a mile away. For example, if I am representing a wife and file a motion for her against a grieving husband who does not want the divorce, he will ensure that every time I file a motion for her, he will file a countermotion – even when it does not make logical sense to do so. These delay tactics can drag things out like you would not believe!

Another indication that lawyers can see coming are passive-aggressive tactics meant to drag out a divorce. This occurs when one of the spouses does not want the divorce but refuses to actively fight it. Instead of saying that they won't do something, they just won't do it. For example, the spouse that filed for divorce will say, "Let's go to mediation so that we can get to the bottom of this and reach a quick conclusion." The other spouse will agree to go, but will refuse to agree on a mediator and or they will never give an open date; they just leave things hanging in the air. Once we are able to finally pin the resistant spouse down on a mediator they begin to resist scheduling a firm date for mediation, the spouse will insist that any date selected is not a good one for him/her because of some conflicting obligation. Then, we propose multiple dates, neither of those dates are good either. Then, we ask, "Can you provide us with a date that will work with your schedule?" The spouse agrees to provide a date but never follows through with the scheduling. These are passive-aggressive delay tactics.

When grieving spouses really want to be obtrusive or resistant, they will even fight the process of mediation itself, even though it is legally required in most states. Thus, we have to take them to court in order to get the judge to rule that they have to go to mediation. Once your motion to go to mediation is granted, you can expect to possibly go through several rounds of back and forth negotiations to determine a date within the range provided by the court. Then, once the date is agreed upon, resistant spouses might fight you on which mediator you choose if one was not appointed by the judge; no one that you choose is good enough for them. Then, you will ask them to choose the mediator, and after several weeks, no response. Again, these passive-aggressive delay tactics are meant to hold onto a relationship because, in their grief, they refuse to accept the fact that things are over and that it's time to move forward.

You might be wondering what the lawyer's role is in all of this. "Does the lawyer realize that the client is using him/her to delay things and drag them out?" The answer is oftentimes yes. Lawyers are professionals, and they can determine very clearly when they are dealing with a client that simply refuses to let go. However, lawyers work for the client, and if the client does not want the divorce, they work to keep the client in that space. Yes, I said it: they help their clients drag out the process as long as they can. The lawyers often willingly allow themselves to be used as a tool, charging their clients along the way. This is where law and emotion run afoul with one another.

Ultimately, whether you are the spouse that wants the divorce or the spouse that is resistant to it, you will both pay the cost when a party drags out the process. Again, divorcing can be quick and easy, but if a grieving spouse is operating out of emotion, it can take seemingly forever to get resolved. In fact, I have seen divorces that could have taken 60 days (the minimum amount of time required by Texas law on a no-fault divorce) take more than three years! Ultimately, if one partner is strongly determined to end things, no one benefits by dragging out the process, for the end of the relationship is inevitable.

In sum, to use your time most efficiently when you go through a divorce, keep in mind the following tips:

1. Know where you are in working through the five stages of grief so that you can stay keenly aware of how these emotions might be making you prone to dragging things out.

2. Don't drag things out. Accept the situation, cut your losses, and move on (especially if you realize that you are the resistant spouse).

3. The value of wasted time is just as significant as that of wasted money.

4. Accept the fact that the longer things drag out the more emotionally taxing and difficult it is for everyone to start over and move forward.

5. When the process is prolonged, it can potentially destroy any possibility of having some kind of pleasant, cordial interaction with one another in the future.

Impact 3: It Can Make You as Irrational as a Child Who is Afraid to Sleep Because of the Boogey Man!

It should be understood that emotion and rationality are two different things. Emotions are based upon what we are feeling; rationality is based upon logical thought and reasoning. Emotions often do not take into consideration the ramifications or impact of the decisions made on an outcome or whether something makes sense or not; thus, they are not perceived as rational. These choices may not "make sense", because instead of coming out of our mind, they come out of our heart and when our heart is hurting our choices often aim at hurting. Oftentimes, one cannot operate out of both emotion and rational thought at the same time; you are usually either operating out of one or the other at any given time.

When you are going through the process of grief, it is easy to fall into the trap of operating out of your emotions, allowing how you feel to govern your words and actions. Especially when you are mentally exhausted and your emotions are raging, a lot of times, it is easier to give way to them rather than fighting them. Thus, even though you might logically know what you should do, you yield to your emotions instead and go with what you feel.

For example, have you ever dealt with a child who was convinced that there was a "boogey man" in the closet? You turned on the light for the child, let him look in the closet, moved all of the contents out of the way to show him that there was nothing hiding in the closet, and even tried to convince him that the boogey man was not real. After all, he had never seen this fictitious monster, so there was no actual evidence that he was real. In his rational thought, he knew that there was no boogey man; however, inside his emotion was a fear – an irrational one – that was so great that he refused to sleep with the lights off at night. This might appear silly to us as parents, but we operate the same way when we choose to follow our emotions instead of our rational thought.

I have seen this happen time and time again when dealing with clients in the midst of a divorce. There have been cases in which I have clearly and repeatedly told my clients what the law said about a particular area. While they understood these things logically, they were not trying to operate out of logic; because they had not worked through the process of grief, they insisted on operating out of emotion.

For example, I had one client who was going through a divorce from her husband, and she was entrenched in the emotions of fear and grief. She was fearful of the unknown, of having to start a new life, of not having enough money, of losing her friends, of living alone, – many of the things that people tend to fear, when dissolving a marriage. This same client was grieving not the loss of her spouse, but the loss of status, her home, her neighborhood, their mutual friends – again, the typical things that people tend to grieve when going through divorce.

One thing, however, that this client was not willing to grieve was the loss of her church. Because of this, she directed me to tell her husband that she would get their church membership; he had to leave. As much I tried to explain that there was no basis in the law for telling her husband that he could no longer worship at their church, she was passionately insistent! In fact, she was so adamant that this clause be written into the divorce paperwork that she refused to move forward with the divorce until he agreed to move his membership to another church! Again, there was absolutely no rational, legal basis for her to do this, but in her grief-stricken emotion, she was going to make it happen. Eventually, she was able to get her way and have it written into the document as a clause during mediation. However, if he decided to violate her "rule" and walk into their church the next day, there would not be a thing that the authorities or the court could do to enforce the order.

In another case that comes to mind, my client allowed her grief to be expressed as greed, an emotion that could have cost her dearly in the end. This client was a woman who wanted everything: the boat, the car, the planet – the world! Her husband not only agreed to give her all of this, but she also got more than 50% of his retirement account, a paid off car, a timeshare vacation property, and rental property. He walked away with little to nothing of the marital estate and was more than gracious to her. However, even though he had given her the lion's share of all they had, she still wanted more!

In an attempt to get her to operate out of logic, I told her that she should recognize how great her settlement was and stop while she was ahead. I showed her the other side of the law: he had allowed her to have all of this without ever going to court, but if she insisted on going to court to get more, she could lose what she had! The rational-thinking person would have been happy with the settlement, celebrated, and moved on with the process. However, she was not operating out of rationality or logical reasoning, she was operating out of grief and hurt. As such, although she already had a larger share of their financial resources, she still wanted more and more. In fact, even though he had given her most of his money which he had acquired before and during the marriage, she insisted I propose to his counsel that he pay all of her bills for the next 18 months. Why? Because she did not want him to have funds available to pay the bills of another woman! Even though he'd paid over and above what was required for his freedom, this still was not enough for her. Had I not been able to convince her to stop her fight while she was ahead, she could have taken him to court for more and lost much of what she'd already gained.

Be careful when you choose to operate out of your feelings of grief rather than your logical, rational mind, because it could cost you dearly!

In sum, to ensure that you are operating out of a rational mind versus your emotions when you go through a divorce, keep in mind the following tips:

1. Know where you are in working through the five stages of grief so that you can stay keenly aware of how the stage you are in can overtake your rational thought process.

2. Be sure that you can pinpoint the difference between when you are processing and operating out of your feelings of grief rather than out of rational thinking.

3. When you have doubts about whether you are being rational or not, just ask your lawyer. He/she will be glad to let you know!

4. Do not allow yourself to make any decisions during times that you are flooded with grief or any other negative emotion.

5. Listen to your lawyers: if they say that something is not lawful, believe them and heed their instructions in order to ensure the best outcome.

Impact 4: It Can Send the People Closest To You Running when They See You Coming!

When you are living in the midst of grief that is not adequately addressed, not only can it cost you time, money, and rationality, it can cost you something even more valuable than any of these: relationships. The relationships that grief-stricken soon-to-be divorcees impact are not only those with the impending ex-spouse, but those with children, extended family members, and friends as well.

Because divorce is such a life-shattering event that most people have never dealt with before, they want to talk about it… over and over and over again. During these discussions, they often desire to talk about their hurt, their confusion, their pain… their grief. While their friends and family members are usually prepared to be there for them in the beginning, they could potentially tire of repeatedly having the same conversation, as after a while, it can become emotionally draining. As a result, when divorcees are ready to re-hash the who's, what's, where's, when's, and why's of the divorce – yet again – over time, the number of friends and family members willing to sit through it becomes fewer and fewer.

Invariably, because they have not dealt with their grief, people going through divorce can be interpreted as "needy" by friends and family members who expect that at some point, they will "get over it". If you have been through a divorce, you know that doing such a thing is more difficult that it would seem. However, at some point, a person has got to come to terms with where they are and move on! If one does not deal with their grief and make some progress, whenever their friends and family see them coming, they might run the other way because they find the stagnant person toxic, negative, and depressing!

Some of the most innocent people with whom parties share relationships can become casualties when they does not deal adequately with the grief of divorce – the children. If you never had a reason to deal with your grief before, consider the fact that these little people need you now more than ever before. Your children did not ask for this divorce; it was thrust upon them. Their lives have changed as much as yours. Their hearts are hurting as much as yours. They are just as confused as you. They are going through a sense of grief of their very own.

The last thing your children need to see is one of the two people that they love the most in life – their parents – fighting, angry, bitter, or in a constant state of grief. They need to know they can come to you for comfort, to feel safe and secure, and to feel stable in a situation that has all-of-a-sudden, unexpectedly become unstable. If you will be fit to effectively parent your children through this situation so that they can survive it with their trust, esteem, and emotions intact, you are going to have to get a handle on your grief and pull yourself together. If not, at the very time when your children will need to run to you, they also will turn and run the other way.

While you should be careful not to leave your children out during this difficult process, I also offer a very important warning to parents: do not drag your children into your divorce! Many times, people will use children as messengers or even as pawns during the divorce process, especially if one spouse is having a difficult time letting go of the other. This is a horrible thing to do!

For example, one of my clients, a woman who was having a hard time letting go, would make up unnecessary issues that needed to be discussed with her husband concerning the kids, just so she could have a conversation with him; he had no desire to speak with her otherwise. There are also other things that are typical of people who use their kids to stay connected to their spouses like making it difficult for the other parent to pick up the kids for visitation, ensuring that they are always present to have a conversation with the other parent when pick-ups and drop-offs occur, plotting and staging situations in which the other parent has to share the same space in the place with them, with or without the presence of the children.

For example, I had one client who was supposed to have her son at home for his dad to pick up for the weekend. The dad showed up at the designated time to pick up his son, but he was not at home. He called the mother, and she explained that she took him to a local restaurant to have a little lunch.

Then, she proceeded to invite the dad to the restaurant to have lunch with them – as a family – so that afterward, he could take the son for the weekend. She was trying to get her soon-to-be ex-husband in the same space at the same place. Needless to say, he said, "No." I'm sure that the child was aware of the manipulation that was transpiring, and it could not have made him feel good to see his mom manipulate his dad. Whatever you do, remember that children are not pawns, and leave them out of your adult interactions.

In sum, to ensure that you do not destroy your relationships when you go through a divorce, keep in mind the following tips:

1. Know where you are in working through the five stages of grief so that you can stay keenly aware of how the stage you are in can affect your relationships.

2. If your need to talk about your grief outlasts your friends' patience, look into hiring a professional counselor to help you work through your grief.

3. Instead of always talking to your friends and family about how bad things are, share with them the hope that you have in your heart for a better future. It will help them to see that you are not getting stuck in the past or continuing to lament the present.

4. Be intentional about pulling yourself together so that you can be emotionally present for your children.

5. Never, ever, ever use your children as messengers, pawns, or tools of manipulation.

Impact 5: It Can Shift Your Focus from the Bottom Line to Getting "The Big Payback"!

As if all of the other ways that grief can impact your life as you go through divorce are not enough, there is more! If you do not get a handle on your grief, it can really get you misfocused! Instead of focusing on the bottom line – splitting up your stuff and ending the relationship – you will be misfocused in your pursuit of something else: the big payback!

There is something about the end of a marriage (especially when one spouse leaves the other) that makes people dead set on making this person that they once loved more than life feel a great deal of pain. Instead of pouring their energies into the goal of dissolving the marriage, they pour their energies into things like hurting the other person, vindication, and exacting sweet revenge.

Something that I have realized over years of working with divorce clients is that there is something that people often want over and above money: they want to be vindicated. They want the world to know that the divorce is not their fault so that they can save face among their family, friends, church members, co-workers, and in the community. The truth is that when a marriage ends, someone is always at fault; someone failed. They want the world to know that this "someone" is not them, and they can only do this by establishing that the public blame goes on their spouse. While they do this for public perception, they ultimately want to be able to face themselves in the mirror and utter those five small, yet meaningful words: It was not my fault.

Then, there are those who want to go beyond assigning blame; they want their spouse to feel some pain! As such, they do all they can to make their soon-to-be ex-spouse's life miserable. I recall one client, a husband, who was adamant that he no longer wanted to be married to his wife, but he maintained a singular focus on hurting her; he'd accepted the fact that they were not going to be together, but he wanted to get his final jabs in during the process.

This husband did not want any money; he just wanted to penalize his wife by asking the judge to put on public record that she had committed marital fraud! Mind you, in Texas (which is where the case was tried), there is no such thing as marital fraud, there is constructive fraud and actual fraud, but he could not prove either had occurred; however, he wanted a written record that specifically detailed that his wife was a liar, thief, and a cheat, and that the divorce was completely her fault! Despite both his legal counsel and the judge trying to explain to him that there was no way to make this a part of the record, he persisted. He kept us in the courtroom for *two hours* trying to get something put on the record that would blemish his soon-to-be ex-wife's character forever! Needless to say, it was never put on the record, and he was quite angry. In fact, he is still stuck in anger to this very day!

I've seen pain-seeking situations like this occur time and time again, but here is something else that I see: each time it happens, the one that is focused on revenge ultimately loses. My best advice to clients who seem to be bent towards "the big payback" is to get what they can get, cut their losses and move on! What they are pursuing out of their grief is simply not worth it!

In sum, to ensure that you are keeping your focus on the bottom line of dissolving your marriage and splitting your assets when you go through a divorce, keep in mind the following tips:

1. Know where you are in working through the five stages of grief so that you can stay keenly aware of how the stage you are in can affect your ability to focus on the bottom line.

2. Keep your eye on the prize: the end of the marriage and a equitable division of your marital property.

3. If you think that you might be focused on getting "the big payback" on your soon-to-be ex-spouse, ask your lawyer to help keep you focused on the matter at hand: getting the divorce finalized.

4. Be intentional about making peace with your soon-to-be ex-spouse. If this is not possible, try at the very least to have neutral interactions with him/her.

5. Remember that the hurt and pain that you cause others will ultimately come back to affect you!

Deal with Your Grief So You Can Move Ahead With Class!

While I could tell story after story about how grief negatively impacts the lives of my clients, this does not have to be the case in your situation. If you choose to properly deal with your grief, there is hope for you to achieve a much better outcome!

There is one story in particular that I believe is a great example of how to deal with your grief and navigate your divorce process in a peaceful and classy way. This client was a woman whose husband had left her – for another man. Needless to say, she was under a great deal of grief when she first came to my office. However, instead of utilizing me as her counselor, she allowed me to deal with the facts, and she sought out professional counseling for herself. She wanted to deal with her grief in a private and professional manner as she tried to wrap her mind around such a devastating event.

Additionally, despite what her husband had done, she left his relationship with his children completely in-tact. She kept the fighting down and engaged in peaceful interaction with him for their sake. In fact, when her husband moved out of the house, she made it fun for all by ensuring that she and the children helped daddy "set up his own place". Throughout the entire divorce process, she maintained a very positive and nurturing attitude towards everyone in the family.

Though this woman was undoubtedly in a great deal of grief, she was able to handle her divorce in a peaceful and classy way. She exemplified the very definition of grace under grief. We can learn several lessons of what to do during the divorce process from her example.

- Lesson 1: Get professional counseling so that you can deal with your grief, and leave the law for the legal experts.

- Lesson 2: Strive to keep peace with your soon-to-be ex-spouse as you work to dissolve the union.

- Lesson 3: Always uphold your soon-to-be ex-spouse as a parent in the eyes of the children, because even though he/she will no longer be your spouse, he/she will always be the parent of your children.

- Lesson 4: Maintain a positive outlook throughout the process, and you will always come out ahead!

- Lesson 5: Remember that even though you are standing your ground and fighting, you can do so with dignity!

In the end, even though it hurts more than you ever imagined it would, it appears that you are going through divorce. Since you have to do it, why not do it with class? Keep your head up, and cast your eyes ahead to look forward to the future instead of backwards to the past. Deal with the grief of where you are, and know that it will not last forever. There is hope after hopelessness, and there are life and joy after grief.

Now that you have a greater understanding of grief and how not having a handle on it can impact your case, the upcoming chapters will help you deal with your grief so that you can:

1. Understand where you are in the five stages of grief:
   - Denial
   - Anger
   - Bargaining
   - Depression
   - Acceptance

2. Negotiate the challenges of that stage of grief

3. Move to navigating the next stage of grief

4. Eventually complete your process of grief – because it does have an end!

A Prayer for Direction…

Before moving on to the next chapter, pray this prayer aloud:

Lord, thank you for knowledge and understanding of the grief process. Thank You for letting me know that I am not alone. Help me to rest in You when I am feeling down and burdened with the grief and pain of divorce. When I am so hurt that all I can do is cry, allow Your Spirit to comfort me, and when I am in so much pain that I do not feel I can continue another step, please strengthen me and help me to continue throughout my process. Though I acknowledge that I am in grief, I also acknowledge that Your word is true: that weeping may endure for a night, but joy comes in the morning. Therefore, Lord, help me to continue pressing through my night knowing that morning is on the way. Amen!

CHAPTER THREE

The Stage of Denial:
"This Can't *Possibly* Be Happening to *Me*!"

The first stage of loss and grief is one in which people have a very difficult time accepting the reality of what is actually occurring in their life. After all of the time, energy, investment, shared experiences, hard work, and intimate moments with their partner, what they have seen happen to so many other marriages is finally happening to their own: it is ending in divorce. *Or is it? No, it can't be.*

For so long, they thought their relationship was immune – impervious, and airtight – to anything that other "lesser" relationships were unable to withstand. In their mind, they were going to be together forever. They had ups and downs, but this is no different from every other relationship, right? They might have to work through some things, but surely, these issues were not pre-requisites for divorce, were they? *This can't be happening. My partner is overreacting, and once they come to their senses, all of this will be over, and we can go back to our life together.*

Can't we?

When the reality of a prospective divorce is introduced, they are now faced with the reality that more than half of all marriages face in the U.S.: sometimes, it doesn't last forever. Like so many others, their marriage is about to become a statistical casualty. The man or woman they loved, the family they created, the home they established together, and the life they built together, are all coming to an end. Regardless of whose fault it was, they have failed at sustaining what is perhaps one of the most basic institutions on earth: marriage. *People have been keeping marriages together since the beginning of time, and yet I couldn't do it. But wait... I can keep mine together, and I will. This divorce isn't happening. I'm not going to let it happen.*

The idea of facing the reality of an impending divorce can be so utterly unbelievable, so unfathomable, so immeasurably inconceivable that some people cannot bring themselves to accept that something so tragic is happening in their life. *It must be a dream,* they say.

I'm going to wake up from this nightmare, and everything is going to be okay, they hope.

If I don't think about it and don't pay any attention to it, everything will pass over, they think.

Impossible! This can't possibly be happening to me! they exclaim.

I had a client who was married for over 25 years. For more than 10 years, she and her husband had not been intimate. He was still very much attracted to his wife and always wanted to try new and different things during their intimate moments, but she was uninterested – so much so that they soon began sleeping in separate bedrooms. In her mind, she was completely convinced that they still had a whole marriage. If you asked her, she would tell you that they were still the best of friends and everything was just fine. However, eventually, he filed for divorce. As her attorney, I would continually ask her why her husband was filing for divorce. She would say that she didn't know; she had no idea. In fact, she was sure that this divorce was not actually happening. After all, she took care of him and did not think he could take care of himself. They shared a home, a family, land, animals, and a life together, so in her mind, this was not actually about to happen. However, it did happen. He was unwavering, and he proceeded with the divorce. She maintained her position of denial all the way through the divorce and even after he signed the divorce decree. Her denial was at such a high level that her children had to intervene to make her understand that this *was* happening – indeed, it already *had* happened – and had to help her move on with her life.

I had another client who was in such denial about her husband filing for divorce that she acted as though she was not divorced, even after the divorce was finalized. She continued to sleep on "her side of the bed" after her husband moved out. She continued to write checks for charities and donations as if it was from the couple. Some mornings, she would even lay out the newspaper and fix breakfast like he was coming to the table to eat. Out of her denial, she continued everything in her life like he was still there – like her marriage had not actually ended. As her attorney, I was interested in her being able to move forward, so I would tell her to take baby steps.

For example, she would still only park on "her side of the garage", so I encouraged her to take the baby step of parking in the middle of the garage. She simply would not park in the middle. She thought that at any moment, her husband would show up at the house, and he would be angry when he opened the garage door because she was parked in the middle of the garage!

Even after the divorce was finalized, she was still in denial, parking in "her spot". However, more than a month after the divorce was over, she sent me an e-mail: "I parked in the middle of the garage!"

What Does a Client in the Midst of the Denial Stage Look Like?

People who are in the stage of denial are some of the most challenging clients for a lawyer to work with for a variety of reasons. As a result of the difficulty they are having accepting that the divorce is actually happening:

- They tend to not provide those providing them with representation the information needed to do their job, which makes it very difficult for their lawyers to strategize on their behalf.

- When their lawyers call or e-mail them, they do not e-mail back.

- The lawyer's office has to spend extra time hounding them for a response, and when they finally do respond, they act as though they never got any of the messages.

- Instead of helping their lawyers build a case for the divorce, they'd rather take an ostrich approach, burying their head in the sand and acting like the divorce is not happening (this makes the lawyer's job *very* difficult to do).

- They tend to acquiesce to everything the spouse wants in the settlement, thinking that if they do, their spouse will come back.

- They continue to act as though they are married, making it difficult to build a divorce case to terminate the marriage.

The Legal Disadvantages of Operating in Denial

When my clients are having a difficult time dealing with the reality of their divorce, I try to encourage them to have the courage to accept where they are and what is happening. Again, grief and every stage associated with it – including denial – is normal. However, not being aware of how operating in denial can affect a divorce case can be harmful.

Regularly, people in denial tend to not make things readily accessible for their lawyers, because they are still convinced that building a case for divorce is not necessary. Remember: in their minds, it can't be happening. Unfortunately by not providing what the lawyer needs to build a case, they put themselves at risk of losing out in court. Though their partner is working with an attorney to strategize against them, they are not willing to strategize against their partner, putting themselves at a legal disadvantage.

When you hire a lawyer to represent you, all your lawyer can ultimately get out of court for you (besides the kids, if you are fighting for custody) is money and assets – a fair division of your shared estate. If you are in denial and not providing your lawyer with every piece of information that could possibly be used to get your fair share of the estate, you lose… sometimes miserably!

For example, a client in denial might not share where her husband's retirement fund is or where his investment accounts are, because she does not want to ask for any of these monies as part of the settlement; she doesn't want to take the chance of making him angry, because she does not want the divorce anyway. In doing so, she hurts her own case. Another client might say that she only wants a meager amount of child support, even though she is legally entitled to much more; again, she wants to stay on her husband's "good side", hoping that this "divorce thing" will pass over if she makes things easy for him. What she does not realize is that by reducing or denying the monies that are legally due to her to care for her children, she is not helping the husband, she is hurting the children. She is reducing her children's ability to do things, go places, and participate in activities that require resources!

Trying to build a case for a client who is in denial and, for all intents and purposes, is working against you can be quite frustrating! Over the years, I have seen many a lawyer actually fire their clients for this major reason: the case was not working because the client was not cooperating with the lawyer. Ultimately, this ends up hurting clients, because they have to now start all over with a new lawyer and they must pay a new retainer. And just in case you're wondering, the answer is no: you do *not* get your retainer monies back if you are fired by your lawyer! Therefore, for your own sake, when you hire a lawyer to represent you in a divorce, cooperate, cooperate, cooperate!

Spiritual Guidance for the Soul in the Stage of Denial

It does no good to provide you with guidance about how to operate in legal matters while in the stage of denial without providing you with some spiritual guidance about how to work through things. Because denial is the first stage of grief, for many, it is often the hardest to overcome. It takes real spiritual effort to deal with the feelings of loss, failure, and hurt that accompany this stage.

If you are in this stage, I believe that what you need most is encouragement to face your situation and yourself. This is indeed happening to you – acceptance is imperative. This present life circumstance does not make you a terrible person, and it doesn't mean that you are any less in worth or significance than any other person walking the earth because you are experiencing a divorce. As a child of the King you belong to God, He says in Deuteronomy 28:13 that *The* LORD *will make you the head, not the tail. If you pay attention to the commands of the* LORD *your God that I give you this day and carefully follow them, you will always be at the top, never at the bottom.* Be encouraged! You are the head and not the tail, and You are above and not beneath, You are a winner – even in the *midst* of a divorce! You are still the wonderful, respectable, valuable, and highlyesteemed person you were before the decision was made to separate from your partner. Don't let the reality that your marital situation is changing alter your self-esteem or your perception of who you are in God.

God has not forgotten you in the midst of this terrible circumstance. He loves you and cares for you. In fact, because you belong to Him, the bible says that anyone who touches you *touches the apple of His eye* (Zechariah 2:8). Be encouraged that despite everything going on around you, God still loves you more than ever, and you are precious and valuable to Him. Therefore, you can face the reality of what is happening with your relationship with the full assurance that it has not changed things between you and God.

Finally, when you are at your weakest point and do not feel like you have the strength to face your situation or yourself, remember this scripture from Philippians 4:13: *I can do all things through him who gives me strength.* This is a scripture that you would do well to memorize and repeat over and over again to encourage yourself when no one else is around to be your encourager. Once you embrace it, you will recognize that you can endure the process of divorce and everything that comes along with it, because you are not doing it out of your own strength but the strength of the Lord!

A Prayer for Direction…

Before moving on to the next chapter, pray this prayer aloud:

Lord, help me to have the boldness, courage, and confidence to accept the reality of where I am. When I feel too weak and vulnerable to accept and deal with the truth of what might be happening, speak to my heart. Give me the strength to face things head on instead of operating in denial. Remind me by Your Spirit that I can do all things through Christ who strengthens me. I know that I cannot do this alone, but with You, I can do all things. Amen!

CHAPTER FOUR

The Stage of Anger:
"I HATE You and EVERYTHING About You!"

The second stage of loss and grief is the stage of anger. This is the stage when, mentally, it all hits the fan! During the stage of anger, people stop feeling sorry for their partner. Instead, they have accepted that the divorce is actually happening, and they are mad as heck! In some cases, they are angry that the person they loved and trusted to be a consistent, forever lifetime partner has changed right before their very eyes, making a divorce necessary. In others, they are angry that their partner didn't seem to care enough or work hard enough on the relationship to keep it together. Some are angry that their partner was not disciplined enough to stay committed to them in a relationship or mature enough to resist being enticed by other men or women instead of being loyal to them.

There are a million reasons about which people in the stage of anger find to be angry. Regardless of the reason they use to justify their anger, however, the outcome is still the same: they live in a constant state of resentment, outrage, and irritation that affects not only them, but everyone around them. In some cases, their tempers are volatile, because this abiding state of anger is always simmering right beneath the surface, just waiting to be provoked – and then it unleashes! In other cases, their tempers are equally volatile, but its expression comes out differently when it is tapped, manifesting in a silent, seething, sarcastic, rage!

There is a difference between living in an abiding state or stage of anger versus experiencing a momentary reaction of anger to something that has happened. A momentary reaction of anger to something undesirable happening is normal; its effects last as long as the moment of anger, and then they fade. However, living in a constant state or stage of anger detrimental to your health and wellness. Why? Because anger impacts a person mentally, physically, and emotionally for as long as the state lasts. In the case of divorce, this could be months – even years!

People who are operating in the stage of anger in a divorce can easily be picked out of the bunch. When you say their partner's name, their eyes immediately start to roll, their head begins to shake back and forth, and their expression says, "Whatever! I can't *stand* him/her!" They haven't an ounce of positive regard about their soon-to-be ex. At the very mention of the name of this person to whom they have affixed some, if not all of the blame for this tragic situation that has turned their life upside down, you can see the hairs on the back of their neck stand up as their face turns another color of crimson. If you look a little more closely than that, you might even see faint puffs of smoke coming out of their ears. They are angry, and when they go through divorce they are out to repay hurt for hurt – and to destroy!

I recall one particular client who was so angry during her divorce that she went to the bank and cleaned out the entire bank account – except for a dollar. When she was asked to justify her actions, she explained that when her husband came into the marriage, all he had was a dollar, and now that he was leaving, this was all he was taking! Of course, the law requires that a couple have a just and right division of all of their marital assets; by law, she could not zero him out by taking all of the money. In fact, the court could have given a punitive decision if she'd refused to share the assets that they had acquired. In any case, she was so angry at her husband that she refused to put the money back, and as a result, I was in court constantly. Unfortunately for her, she was not the only one that was angry; the judge grew angry because I could never get her to compromise her position about the money! Eventually, my client found a way around having to share the money with her husband. The law says that people can choose to spend their money on a business and on legal fees. In light of this, my client, again out of her anger, invested the money into her business and *intentionally* made bad business decisions so that there would be fewer assets to split. She depleted a *significant* amount of their resources just so her husband could not get his hands on very much of anything! However, I continued to remind her that she was not only depleting his assets; she was also depleting her own.

Another client, a man who knew he was about to get divorced, was also angry. In fact he was so angry, he wanted to make sure his wife would not get any of "his" money in the divorce: he completely cleared all of the money out of his retirement account and paid cash to buy a brand new seven series BMW. Understanding that he did this to keep his wife from getting her hands on the money as part of the settlement, I advised him that he should not have done this, because his wife could just ask for the car in the settlement. A week later, he wrecked the car. Though it was not totaled, it was damaged to the point that it could not be driven. Then, he began driving his old little beat-up pick-up truck throughout the rest of the divorce. Of course, when we negotiated the settlement, because of its diminished value, his wife did not want the BMW. In my heart, however, I knew he had wrecked the car intentionally, and it was all a result of his anger.

There was yet another client who was operating out of anger whom I'll never forget. We were deeply involved in the middle of her divorce case, and then I found out something that no lawyer likes to discover: she was withholding information from me. As a result of the information she was holding back, we lost the trial – miserably! It disturbed me that I had asked her repeatedly, if there was any additional information that she had not shared with me, but she insisted that she had disclosed it all. In reality, she was so angry at her husband she wanted to keep him from having access to some personal assets in the estate that she was "hiding". Once we got to court, she finally disclosed some of these things, but by then, it was too late.

Once her husband's attorney found out about them, he went after them, and this cost her *dearly*. If she had only told me about everything beforehand, we could have protected it; but out of her anger, part of her revenge was to not give her husband the satisfaction of sharing some of her personal assets! What was even worse is that when these hidden things came out in court, the judge pierced me with a visual scolding suggesting, "You should have known about these things!" Now it was my turn to be angry – and so embarrassed! The next time a client came to me for a case and did not want to expose information, I turned her away. I declined to take the case, because I was *not* going to relive that experience ever again!

What Does a Client in the Midst of the Anger Stage Look Like?

People who are in the stage of anger are easily identifiable as soon as you push the right button – and the "right button" just happens to be any topic that is even remotely associated with their ex-spouse. When clients are operating out of anger:

- They tend to be extremely sharp, cutting, and biting.

- They are generally unpleasant with lots of negative energy.

- When working with their lawyer, they are extremely resistant and unwilling to cooperate or negotiate.

- They tend to blame everything on the other person and do not see their role.

- They tend to be deceptive and deny things.

The Legal Disadvantages of Operating in Anger

A lawyer has to really be careful when working with a client who is operating out of anger, because they can be so caught up in their emotions that they become blinded to rational thinking. This, in turn, not only hurts them but those around them.

The first way that operating out of a sense of anger can put a client at a disadvantage has already been discussed, and it is quite common among angry clients: deception, or the tendency to hide things. Their anger causes them to operate out of a sense of spite, bitterness, and resentment to the point that they will do "whatever it takes" to keep their spouse from the perception of winning in court, including being deceitful.

Once, during the discovery period, I gave my client a questionnaire to fill out that included providing a list of his assets, and he returned it to me virtually empty. Puzzled, I asked him why he did not list the information; from our initial conversation, I knew that he had much more, and these things were missing from the questionnaire. His reply was that he wanted me to have plausible deniability as his lawyer, which is a fancy way of saying that he was withholding the information from me to protect me from repercussions in the event that the information became known by the court.

Needless to say, I didn't take the case. It is one thing to be angry, but it is yet another to be deceptive. It is one thing to be angry, but it is another thing to knowingly put my law license on the line!

People going through divorce tend to think that deception will help them to win in the end; however, the opposite is what usually happens. The court is not very kind to those whom it discovers to be operating in deception. When a judge realizes that a client has not been completely forthcoming, this could cost the client dearly – especially financially!

The court is also not very friendly to those who use their children as pawns – negotiating instruments or tools of manipulation – against the other parent during the divorce process. Unfortunately, angry parents often use this heinous tactic. If the court discovers that your anger is thwarting the relationship between the children and the other parent and you are the parent who has custody of the children, it can change the custody of the children to the other parent! If you are engaging in these tactics as the noncustodial parent, the court can limit your access to your children!

Another thing that the court does not like – but is unfortunately accustomed to dealing with – is the games that angry parents play. For example, some angry parents will be completely inflexible and uncompromising when it comes to parental visitation. If the court orders that the father, for example, is supposed to pick up his children from a designated place at 6 pm, and he is one minute late, the mother will not let the father pick the children up, claiming that he violated the court order by being late! Again, the court does not like these angry-parent games. When you play them, you risk losing custody of your children simply because the court does not want children to live in such an angry and manipulative environment.

For example, in one case, the wife of my client was a woman who was over the top bitter and angry at her husband during the divorce process. She had custody of their son, and the court order for visitation allowed the father to pick the little boy up from daycare at 3 pm. Though this was the agreed-upon time, the daycare stayed open until 6:30 pm, so there was neither a credit for picking the child up at 3 pm nor an extra charge for waiting until 6:30 to pick up the child. My client would leave his office and drive 45 minutes, through traffic, to the daycare to arrive at 3 pm.

However, if traffic was bad, he might arrive a few minutes after 3 pm. Once he did arrive, the daycare would tell him that his son had already been checked out. It turned out, his mother would sit outside of his daycare at 3 pm, and if she did not see that their son was picked up by 3:10 pm, she would go in, check him out, and take him home. When my client would call her to find out what happened, she would explain to him in her own bitter and verbally and emotionally-abusive way, that he was ten minutes late, so he had forfeited his visitation for the whole weekend.

Of course, this was unacceptable; blocking a loving father from seeing his son because his angry wife was being spiteful was hurting not only the father, but his son. Both the judge and the amicus (the legal representative and court advocate for the child) grew more and more frustrated at the mother, and eventually, her behavior hurt her case and her child in ways she never imagined. Again, the court frowns upon angryparent games like these, because parental alienation is one of the worst things that you can do to a child.

Another thing that the court stands behind is its rule of ordering parents not to talk to their children about the court case. When people are angry, they often allow this negative emotion to block out their sense of reason. One might think that parents could easily see how discussing the ugly realities of a court case could affect – even devastate – their children. However, angry parents do it all of the time. If it were not for the courts protecting the interests of the children and ordering the parents to remain hush about the divorce and custody case, far too many children would hear about unspeakable things that would change their lives forever – for the worse.

Always remember that if you allow anger to overtake you to the point that you launch into how horrible the other parent is, you might feel a sense of release, or you might feel like your children see you as the "better parent". However, the children are still hurt from this because this other person that you are characterizing as no-good, negative, and worthless is a part of them. Thus, when you tell them that one of their parents is bad, it is the equivalent of saying to them that one half of them is no-good, negative, and worthless. Your articulated anger for your spouse can wreak havoc on your children by costing them a great amount of self-image and esteem.

What's more, it could also cost you custody and access to your children in your legal battle.

If you battle with anger during the divorce process, keep this story of one of my clients in mind. This particular client was so angry that her husband was leaving her and moving to another city that she kept insisting that he only be permitted to have visitation with his children once a month. Despite her insistence, the court gave him a complete possession order, which meant that he could have his children on the first and third weekends of the month. This ended up costing her financially. Here's how: even though the father who was moving to another city said that he was willing to take care of all of the transportation costs during his weekend, the court ordered the mother to pay half of the costs of transportation. Why? Because the court is not friendly towards angry parents. If you are going to have a chance at winning your legal battle, you must get a handle on your anger!

Spiritual Guidance for the Soul in the Stage of Anger

It is easy to see why you are having feelings of anger at this point in your life. You never dreamt that you would be here, and now that you are, the sense of grief, loss, and failure are so overwhelming that you can think of no other way to deal with them other than to blame and lash out. However, I am here to tell you that you have a choice. There is another way to deal with things that will leave you with a greater sense of calm and peace and an increased chance of surviving this process with your sanity, your relationships, your mental and physical health, and what's left of your family and friends intact.

At the foundation of what you are feeling in this stage is a refusal to forgive the person who hurt you. Matthew 18:21-22 says, *Then Peter came to Jesus and asked, "Lord, how many times shall I forgive my brother or sister who sins against me? Up to seven times?" Jesus answered, "I tell you, not seven times, but seventy-seven times.* If you are going to operate in obedience to God's word, you must realize that there are no limits on forgiveness! As many times as you are violated by someone, this is the number of times you must forgive. Can you imagine how many times we have violated God, and He has forgiven us time and time again. We ask Him to forgive us because

83

we are flawed, we didn't mean to violate Him, and we won't do it again; but we do, and He forgives us anyway. In the same way that God forgives us, we are to forgive others!

You might say, "But my spouse knows exactly what he/she is doing to me when these things happen, so how can I forgive?" To this, I have two questions for you: When Jesus was on the cross and asked His Father to forgive those who were beating and crucifying Him because "they do not know what they are doing" (Luke 23:34), do you really think that these men were not conscious of the fact that they were beating and crucifying Him? Of course they were! When Jesus said they did not know what they were doing, it was because He knew that they did not know that as they were mocking Him, spitting on Him, whipping Him, tearing out His beard, and nailing Him to the cross that they were doing this to the Son of God. They knew what they were doing on a conscious level, but not a deeper level! This is also true for your spouse, whom you might consider to be constantly antagonizing you. Your spouse knows what he/she is doing on a conscious level, but he or she is probably completely unaware of the deep hurt caused by these words and actions. Therefore, forgive them, for they do not really understand the depths of what they are doing.

For the sake of your own sanity and survival, you must let things go and forgive. Let go of the hurt. Let go of the pain. Let go of the blame. Let go of the sense of failure. Let go of the expectations of others. Let go of the need to hold something against another person. Matthew 18:23-35 shows us the Parable of the Wicked Servant. The servant owed a huge debt to his master that he would never be able to repay, but the master had mercy on him, canceled his debt, and let him go. However, the servant went out and found someone who owed him a little bit of money. When the man cried out to him for mercy, this same servant who had been forgiven had the man thrown into jail! When the master heard about what this man had done – not being merciful enough to extend forgiveness when he had been given forgiveness himself, he had the servant handed over to the jailers to be tortured! The parable ends in verse 35 with Jesus saying, "This is how my heavenly Father will treat each of you unless you forgive your brother or sister from your heart." As hard as it seems, you must be intentional and determined to show the mercy to others that you have received from your heavenly Father. Let it go. In doing so, you don't only free others; you free yourself.

A Prayer for Direction…

Before moving on to the next chapter, pray this prayer aloud:

Lord, deliver me from my anger. Help me to release all blame, bitterness, resentment, and any negative feelings that would cause me to sin against You as I go through this process of divorce. Just as you do not hold my wrongdoings against me, help me not to hold the wrongdoings of others against them. Allow your Spirit to constantly remind me to show love and forgiveness to my spouse, regardless of what happens throughout the legal process. Help me to not carry anything that is not like You in my heart; instead, allow my heart to be filled with the fruit of the Spirit, which is love, joy, peace, patience, kindness, goodness, faithfulness, gentleness, and selfcontrol so that there will not be any room for anger. Thank you, Lord, for your deliverance. Amen!

CHAPTER FIVE

The Stage of Bargaining:
"*If Only* I Had Been a Better Spouse"

The third stage of loss and grief is bargaining. During this stage, the person's thoughts are inundated with "If only's" and "What if's" as they try to either go back in their mind to how things were and fix what they perceived as broken. This stage is characterized by a sense of guilt: guilt of the past for not doing things that could have prevented what is happening from happening. *If only I had been a better spouse. If only I had really listened to my partner, I could have seen this coming and fixed it. What if I had been a more free-spirited and exciting spouse? What if I had never opened up that social media account?*

Over and over, the scenarios of the past are replayed in their mind. They relive the years, months, weeks, and days gone by that led to their spouse deciding to leave. The responses at the times their spouse expressed discontent are repeatedly questioned. The times when their spouse asked them to change a certain behavior are mulled over constantly. The times when they took their spouse for granted and did things that they knew would cause hurt or pain become a source of regret. With each episode of the past comes a list of more "If only's" with which they try to understand where the real breaking point occurred so they can fix the error. However, these flashbacks and their hindsight remedies are to no avail. Most often, they discover that it's simply too late.

The stage of bargaining is also a stage of negotiating for many people; they engage in mental negotiation with a spouse, God, or whoever they consider to be a higher power that can deliver them out of the situation. People in this stage tend to feel a desperate need to negotiate any deal that can stop the pain of today. They promise, *If you make this unbearable pain stop, I promise that I will be a better person.* They bargain, *If you bring my spouse back to me, I will never, ever, ever devalue them again.* They even beg, *Please God, if you will bring my spouse back to me and make them love me again, I will lose weight, I'll make myself more attractive, and I'll never say 'No' when they want to be intimate with me, be adventurous with me or even just converse with me!*

The combination of the guilt from the "What if's" and the desperation of the "If you'll just make it better, I will..." bargains makes people in the stage of bargaining more susceptible to manipulation, exploitation, and even abuse. Unfortunately, when some people see how desperate their grieving spouses are to fix things, they take full advantage of them and the situation for their own gain. It is unethical, unfair, and coldhearted, but it happens all the time. It is especially important to be aware of when people are in this stage; when they are particularly vulnerable to being seduced, double-crossed, and hoodwinked by those who once claimed to love them the most!

Unlike the stage of denial, which ignores the current reality, or the stage of anger, which assigns responsibility for the current reality to the other person, the stage of bargaining is one in which people become more introspective. They have finally reached the point at which they are seeking to find their role in the outcome of the situation and to deal with the guilt that accompanies accepting some level of fault or blame for it. Even though they realize they might not be able to go back in time, fix things, and change their spouse's mind about wanting to divorce, these mental exercises at least provide them with an opportunity to arrive at some sense of acceptance about what they could have done to avoid the situation. Whether their "mental fix" might have worked or not, no one will ever know.

I had one client that had been married for 36 years. She and her husband owned a farm with lots of land. One day, her husband went out and bought a nice riding lawnmower, something he had been wanting for some time and greatly enjoyed. The wife, a stay-at-home mother, wanted to help out and do her part, so she hopped on the lawnmower and cut the grass. The first time she did this, she absolutely loved it and found it to be quite therapeutic. Further, taking care of this responsibility made her feel peaceful, stronger, empowered, and needed. Her husband came home to find the grass cut, and he said, "Oh… you cut the grass already." She proudly replied, "Yes! I don't mind doing it, and I really enjoy it on the riding mower!" Over time, she continued to cut the grass, and he continued to come home and say, "Oh… you cut the grass." Eventually, one day, the husband filed for divorce, seemingly out of nowhere. He said, "I want a divorce, and I want the lawnmower." When she came to me as a client, all she kept saying was, "Why couldn't I just let him cut the grass? I should have let him cut the grass! *If only* I had let him cut the grass, we wouldn't be here!" Over and over again, she would say this. I started wondering, *Is the end of this 36-year old marriage really about the grass?* I decided to call her husband's lawyer to find out. I asked him if we were dissolving a marriage of 36 years because she cut the grass. His reply was, "No. We are divorcing a couple married for 36 years because she emasculated him." In her mind, it was about the grass, but the end of the marriage was actually about something much greater.

I had another client who was married, but she was not domestic. She was the oldest of five children, so growing up, her mother had relied upon her to do just about everything in the house: cooking dinner for the whole family, cleaning, laundry, taking care of the younger kids, keeping them after school, helping them do their homework, and other chores. As a result, she felt like she had been a mother since the age of 12. Eventually, she met a young man while they were both in high school. He knew her as a caretaker of her younger siblings, and he admired this domestic quality in her. Little did he know that she had done these things for so long that by the time she got married, she'd pledged to herself that she was retiring – she was not going to do them anymore. Their house was always a mess, she wouldn't cook, and he had gotten something completely different than he'd expected. After he could not take living like this anymore, he filed for divorce. In his mind, because she had abandoned her domesticated qualities, she reneged on her part of the bargain to be a domesticated wife. When she came to me to represent her in the divorce, she was immersed in "If only's":

If I had only done what I'd always done, I'd still be married. If I had only tried a little harder to be who he needed me to be, I could have kept my husband. Eventually, she was convinced that it was not too late to implement her "If only's", so she changed her behavior: if a domesticated wife was what he wanted, a domesticated wife is what he would get! While the divorce case was going on, she would cook for him. Since they were already separated, he would come over and eat... and then he would leave. She simply could not understand why, now that she was being what he wanted her to be, this was not enough to keep him in the home. However, the new family context that she was trying to create was forced... contrived. By this time, she, the kids, and her husband had all settled into their new and separate routines, so there was no longer a natural family feel. Thus, her attempts to remedy the guilt and regret of the past could not fix her current situation.

What Does a Client In the Midst of the Bargaining Stage Look Like?

It might seem that people who are in the midst of the bargaining stage would be easier to work with than denial or anger, but people in this stage have their challenges, too. Clients who are operating out of this stage are characterized by such behaviors as:

- They tend to give in to whatever their partner wants with hopes that it will bring them back together for reconciliation.

- They are overly-generous, giving more than they have to in the settlement to their partner because they are interested in staying on good terms with the partner.

- They go into a "Let me please you" mode in which they constantly try to please their partner.

- They try to give their partner what they believe he/she wants more than the divorce (based upon the "What if's" they have concluded were the cause of the divorce)

The Legal Disadvantages of Operating in Bargaining

When people are so desperate to save their marriage or win their spouse back, they will do just about anything. Whatever it takes, they will do, as long as it will deliver them from this terrible reality of divorce.

However, I advise my clients to be cautious of the lengths to which they will go to bargain their way out of an inevitable divorce.

I know that losing a soul mate, a life partner, and a best friend in your spouse is devastating. I know that it hurts so much that you would do anything short of cutting off one of your limbs to stop the pain and the potential reality of living without this loved one for the rest of your life. I even know that for most in this situation, you're not too proud to beg. However, you must remember that you are a person who still deserves the respect of yourself and others. If you have children, you must also consider them; give them someone to look up to who displays dignity and selfrespect. At the end of the day, you should only engage in actions that will allow you to look at yourself in the mirror and be able to say to yourself with positive regard, "I still admire and value you highly."

I once had a client who was married to a man that chose to represent himself rather than hiring an attorney. When her husband walked into my office, she was already sitting there. As soon as she saw him, she looked up to him with pleading eyes and said, "I will do anything and everything that you ask to end this divorce." With kindness in his eyes, he looked back at her and said, "I know you would, but if you did, I would love you even less than I do now." In this, he was expressing that he would have no respect for her if she did whatever he wanted, because she would have lost who she was to become what he wanted her to be.

In addition to potentially losing your self-respect when you operate from a sense of bargaining, you could also stand to lose out financially. I was representing the children of a couple as a court-appointed amicus during a custody battle. In the bargaining, the mother was so desperate to gain full custody of the children that she was willing to forego any claims to his retirement account. The husband knew that she desperately wanted custody of the children, so he took advantage of this – manipulated her – in order to get her to give up claims to the retirement account. This would turn out to be a bad move, because she had no ability to recover these assets that would be needed to take care of the children as well as to take care of herself. A few years later, the father came back and fought for full custody of the children in a modification. Here's the bad news: she lost custody of the children because she did not have the money to fight him adequately. Because she had allowed herself to be manipulated into giving up claims to his money in order to keep her children, he could now come back to use what he had deprived her of to get what he initially wanted in the original process. As the court-appointed advocate for the children, this was one of the most hurtful things I have ever had to witness. Because the mother could not afford the legal fees, she ended up representing herself in the modification proceedings. Three years after she had given up all claims to the money, so that her husband would leave the children alone, she lost them to the same deception and manipulation that she had succumbed to in the divorce.

Another client of mine wanted to keep his marriage, even though his wife said that she wanted a divorce. The husband had received some land that had oil on it as a gift from his family. This was separate property (property owned before the marriage or acquired by gift, devise or descent or in limited circumstances through a personal injury settlement) that the court could not divide, so it would clearly be off limits to his wife in the divorce. However, because he was in a stage of bargaining, his goal was to make his wife happy in order to stop the divorce. She told him that if they would have a chance at reconciliation, he would have to sign over the deed for the land to her. He did. And guess what? She went through with the divorce, and his land was gone. He lost something to his wife that even the courts did not have the power to take away!

It is essential to be carefully aware of what emotional stage you are making decisions out of, especially when you think you might be dealing with the stage of bargaining. Why? Because you can easily be manipulated by others who understand your level of desperation to simply end the pain and make life like it was before. Now is the time to be more cautious than ever before, because if you are not, you might end up paying a hefty price with your esteem, your children, your pocketbook, and more!

You can be manipulated in the bargaining process when you are unwilling to see that divorce is eminent. If it looks like a divorce is a sure thing because your marriage can't be reconciled, stand your ground and fight for an equitable distribution. If your relationship is sustainable, it will have to be sustainable outside of the parameters of you having to give up everything about yourself and everything in your bank account to make it work. In cases of divorce where people lose so much, your financial footing might be all that you have left; don't bargain it away out of desperation.

Spiritual Guidance for the Soul in the Stage of Bargaining

People who have reached the stage of bargaining have often already reached out to God, or to the spiritual being or higher power they believe has the power to help them out of their painful situation. However, while they are often focused upon asking for help to make it end, my advice to them would be to ask for something that is of even greater necessity in this stage: protection from those who will prey upon them during such a vulnerable stage and the wisdom to know when they are being manipulated by people that they trust.

If you are to ever get out of the stage of bargaining and reduce your chances of manipulation that accompany it, you must stop living in the past, stop trying to recreate it with a better outcome based upon the "What if?" and "Why didn't I?" questions that you constantly ask yourself and stop giving up who you are and what you have to try and please your spouse. Give yourself a break. Despite what you might be inclined to think, you are not the worst person in the world. You did the best that you could do based upon your knowledge of what to do at the time. Now, deal with the present, and strive towards the future. The past no longer needs your attention, because it is over and gone. However, the future that God has planned for you needs all of the time, energy, and attention that you can give if it is going to come to pass!

Continuing to reflect upon the past – whether it was a good past or a bad past – can be a hindrance to where God wants to take you in your future.

The apostle Paul shows us this in Philippians 3:13-14 when he writes, *Brothers and sisters, I do not consider myself yet to have taken hold of it. But one thing I do: Forgetting what is behind and straining toward what is ahead, I press on toward the goal to win the prize for which God has called me heavenward in Christ Jesus.* Interestingly, Paul said that the one thing that he did was forget the past. You see, he understood that in order to keep pressing and reaching for the prize that God had called him to, he had to forget the past. Dwelling in the past is a hindrance to moving ahead in the things of God. Thus, be mindful to forget the past. Stop questioning it and let it go. Then, reach for the future to which God is calling you!

A Prayer for Direction...

Before moving on to the next chapter, pray this prayer aloud:

Lord, I pray that You would help me to stop living in the past, asking questions about what might have been, and wondering what would have happened if I had done things differently. You know, Lord, what would have actually happened in every scenario that I have imagined, and yet You allowed me to experience the scenario that I am experiencing, so I know that everything is going to work together for my good. Rather than living in what might have been, Lord, help me to forget the past and focus on getting through this process and striving towards the future that You have designed for me. I trust You at Your word – that You have a glorious future in store for me, and I thank You in advance for the testimony that I will have when I reach it! Amen!

CHAPTER SIX

The Stage of Depression: "Nothing in Life *Really* Matters Now… but Sleep"

The fourth stage of loss and grief is one that is usually the first to come to mind when we think of someone going through the process of divorce: depression. The reason that we tend to associate it so closely with divorce is because "depressed" is the umbrella term that we use to characterize people who constantly appear to be down and whose behavior suggests that there is something that is causing an alteration in their lives – a great sadness. The reality is that they might be going through any one of the other stages of loss and grief, but since depression is a term that we tend to be most familiar with, we attribute the majority of these behaviors to a state of depression.

According to Merriam Webster dictionary, the definition of depression as "A state of feeling sad" or "A serious medical condition in which a person feels very sad, hopeless, and unimportant and is often unable to live in a normal way"[III]. If you have ever interacted with someone who is deep in a state of depression, you know first-hand that it is indeed a defining characteristic of those who are depressed to not have the ability to live in a "normal way". In fact, one of the first means by which we identify someone who is depressed is by their changed behavior, which is no longer "normal" for that person.

When you mention their drastic weight change, they say, *I know I'm losing weight, but I can't make myself eat anything.*

[III] "depression." Merriam-Webster.com. 2014. http://www.merriamwebster.com/dictionary/depression

When you try to cheer them up by inviting them out for dinner with the gang, they reply, *What good is it to try to have a good time when there is nothing funny? Life as I know it is over, so what is there to laugh about?*

If they've been sleeping for several days and a friend asks them out for lunch on a pleasant sunny afternoon, they decline, saying, *I'm just going to stay in and sleep. All I want to do is sleep. Nothing else matters anymore.*

When people are depressed, their emotional state often overtakes their ability to function according to life as usual. Usually, these behaviors manifest in extremes. Their eating habits might change: they eat much more or much less than usual. Their sleeping habits might change: they sleep much more or much less than usual. Their work habits might change: they either throw themselves completely into their work or neglect work altogether. Additionally, their social interactions, their exercise habits, their housekeeping rituals, participation in their hobbies, their church attendance, and even their personal maintenance habits might be similarly affected.

It must be said that just as there are stages of loss and grief, there are stages of depression. It is normal and natural for someone who is dealing with divorce to experience the effects of depression; however, when this depression becomes debilitating and has a detrimental affect on one's life, and especially if one is considering harming oneself, it's' time to seek professional help.

I recall one client that I had who came to me about handling her divorce. Her husband had just disappeared without warning all of a sudden, and she did not know where he was anymore. Though she tried to contact him, he had stopped taking her calls and text messages. Every few months or so, he would send her an e-mail saying that he was okay and just needed his space, because he was still trying to "figure things out". Eventually, this got to be too much for her – the yo-yo effect of the emotional ups and downs, the hope and the hopelessness, were making her crazy. She had been extremely stressed out, and she decided that she needed to move on with her life. When this lady came to me, she was a tiny woman, about 5'4" and 120 pounds. She admitted that she had stopped eating, because she was too sad to eat. In fact, she said, she was 245 pounds when this ordeal began one year ago! I figured that she might be exaggerating a little, so of course, I replied, "No way!" She was going to prove it to me: she pulled a few pictures out of her purse and showed them to me while in my office. My mouth dropped open. I was flabbergasted. It was the same beautiful face, but it was a completely different woman! I sat there shocked at how this lady had completely lost an entire person. I remember this story vividly because it was one in which I silently stared in wonder and amazement at the pictures, then up at the lady, then back at the pictures, then up at the lady for about five straight minutes, which is a long time to sit in silent shock in front of someone.

I had another client whose depression really hurt him because it cost him his job. As a result of the depression from his divorce, he completely stopped going to work. Every day, I would receive an e-mail from him asking me if I had heard from his wife that day. I thought this to be odd, repeatedly explaining to him that I had not heard from his wife because there was no reason for her to contact me; she had her own attorney. However, he never received my e-mail responses, because once he e-mailed me, he was so anxious about potentially hearing what he did not want to hear that he would not open my replies. The replies that he would have liked to receive were those from his wife, but she refused to open his emails. Eventually, I needed to know what was going on, so I contacted the wife's attorney. He explained that the wife had already moved on and simply wanted to divide all of the assets – a normal divorce. In fact, he was surprised that we – my client and I – did not already know this information. He followed up with his client, the wife, and she explained that she had not talked to her husband because he had not been doing his visitation with the children. After the other attorney communicated this back to me, I followed up with my client who admitted that this was indeed true. Mind you, it took about three weeks to get a reply from him about the matter. Once he finally returned my call, he said that he had stopped checking his e-mails and voice messages; he had not even contacted his children because they reminded him of his wife. He admitted that he had not left the house for three weeks, and because of this, he had not shown up to work and lost his job. But guess what? He said he didn't care. He said he had a plan: he would file for unemployment, and he would live off of his savings, which turned out to be his credit cards. As his attorney, I encouraged him to get up and pull himself together, because he had children; he said he just couldn't. He proceeded to not leave the house for a full month. He had no food in the fridge; for meals, he would simply order pizza. He was in bad shape. He was ultimately divorced and luckily for him the judge did not alter his visitation schedule, but he came painfully close to a reduction in his court ordered time with the children because during his depression he did not exercise that which had previously been ordered.

What Does a Client in the Midst of the Depression Stage Look Like?
Depression tends to cause a sense of apathy and lethargy to the point that people's minds seem to be in a constant fog, and I can discern this in my clients as soon as they walk into my office for a consultation. Because of their state:

- They show extreme discouragement and or indifference but not anger.

- They cry. A lot.

- Because they are still caught up in the emotion of the demise of the relationship, the initial consultation includes lots of crying rather than communicating information.

- They tend to barely make eye contact, and they look down and doodle all of the time, suggesting that their body is present but their mind is not focused.

- They are very much withdrawn from the technical, legal aspects of the divorce and tend to be passively resistant.

- They are non-responsive when asked for information needed to build a strategy for the divorce case.

- They have often shut down socially, emotionally, and physically, and they have stopped functioning and handling the responsibilities of life; they merely – barely – exist.

When a client is trying to handle a divorce in the middle of a depression, I can always tell that they know working with an attorney is something they need to do, but even though they can pull their bodies into participating in the process, they have a really hard time engaging their mind and emotions in the process. For example, I am paid to move things forward with the business of dissolving the relationship and dividing the marital estate, so I am constantly explaining the facts – even though they are doodling or seem to be lost in space. Then, when I ask them if they understand what I am saying and ask them if they have any questions, they almost always say "No". After I asked one depressed, disengaged client if she had any questions, she looked at me with eyes full of hurt and pleading and asked, "Can you make this go away?" I told her that I could make the marriage go away but not the divorce. Unfortunately, she was never able to overcome her emotional state and engage throughout the entire the divorce.

Those who do ask questions often tend to ask questions that are emotional and not related to the legalities of the case, or they ask legal questions that are overshadowed by emotion. For example, if we receive and offer for a settlement from their spouse's attorney, instead of asking, "Is this the best possible settlement that I can get, considering all of the facts of the case, or should I ask for more?" they ask, "Do we have to respond? What happens if we just do nothing?"

The Legal Disadvantages of Operating Out of Depression

Because of the level of disengagement that tends to characterize clients dealing with depression, I usually have my work cut out for me as their attorney. We are supposed to go through the journey together as lawyer and client, but I typically have to pull them along, coaxing information out of them (because of their passive-resistance), trying to get them to pay attention, working extra hard to help them understand what is going on so they can contribute facts that might help their case. I can usually get them to at least engage at a level to where we get the necessary paperwork filed and get the issue settled in court; however, the outcomes might have potentially been much more favorable if the clients were fully engaged throughout the entirety of the process.

Being immersed in depression without having a handle on it can hurt you during a divorce in several ways. For example, it can make clients lose their edge to the point that they are not savvy concerning the decisions they make during the proceedings. Remember my client that went from 245 pounds to 120 pounds as a result of her depression? Well, the fact that she lost all of this weight as a result of her depression might seem like a good thing – although I wished she would have lost it in a healthier way.

However, in her depression, she didn't quite think things all the way through; she lost her edge, and it came back to bite her. Here's how.

Over the course of the year she spent in depression dealing with her absentee, elusive husband, this lady had stopped eating and socializing with friends, which caused her to have extra money. She thought she was being smart: she took all of this extra money, along with extra money she was getting from a new job she started, and she started a savings and participated in a retirement account. Prior to this, she and her absentee husband had no substantial assets to divide. However, after a year of saving and investing, she learned that she would have to divide these assets with her husband who had not even been a part of the marriage for a whole year! She was already depressed, but hearing this made her even sadder. I recall her saying, "He has already taken so much from me… and now he is still taking."

There is yet another way in which divorce can hurt a depressed client: financially. Remember my depressed client that had stopped visitation with his children and lost his job because he refused to leave his house for a month? His depression also came back to bite him in another major way. Here's how.

I finally got my client to communicate and work with me once I was able to convince him that his wife was moving full steam ahead with the divorce and we had deadlines to meet if we were going to be in compliance with the court. Because he had lost his job as a result of his depression, we listed him as unemployed to establish the level of child support that he would have to pay. However, his wife's attorney was not accepting this present day circumstance. He utilized all of my client's work history, background, and education level to demonstrate to the court that he was indeed employable, and he could be paying much more than what his unemployment would allow him to pay. The judge agreed, while leaving his visitation schedule intact my client was ordered to pay child support that amounted to three times his entire unemployment check even though he was not working! Keep in mind that in Texas, where the court handed down the verdict, failure to pay child support is the only debt that can result in incarceration. In fact, they jail people all of the time for this – for up to six months!

Another example of depression hurting a case legally involved the husband of one of my clients. He was a commercial airline pilot who early during the marriage promoted to flying jets and eventually landed a job flying commercial jets, but because of the depression of the divorce process, he just stopped showing up for flights. He didn't go to work, he didn't fly… he couldn't bring himself to do anything. All of his income dried up, and my client, his wife, was livid! She was a corporate executive, so she made enough money to take care of herself and their children. In the settlement, he ended up giving her all of his retirement monies to make up for the back child support he owed, so he lost out in a big way financially. (In a way, she also lost out, because retirement money is something that you usually access for the future, not that you use to take care of your children's needs today if it can be avoided.) Further, when he finally did go back to work, he lost again: he had to start at the bottom with an entry level position; he had to re-establish trust and credibility in his industry.

Depression also tends to affect my clients' by keeping them from properly planning for their long-term future. As a result of their minds being so clouded, they do not engage in carefully planning their future as a single person or a single parent. For example, if you are a custodial parent, you must plan for where you and your children will live and how you will live on a reduced income. How will you pay your legal fees with such a drastic cut in your resources? It takes a plan.

If you are a non-custodial parent, you must plan to pay for child support, living expenses and your legal fees. How will you do this? It takes a plan. Where will you live when you move out of the family home? Even if you only have visitation with your children for two weekends a month, you must plan to have adequate living arrangements for adults and children, which in the Court's opinion often includes separate sleeping quarters.

I especially have to spend extra time helping my male clients realize that the decisions they make about their future will impact other people in their lives, particularly the children. They tend to look at their income and say, "Oh well, I can't afford to get a two-bedroom apartment after I pay child support." However, I explain to them that the court will want to know that when their children come to visit, they will have a place that they can call "home". If children visit their father for the weekend and have to sleep on the couch, this does not feel like home for them. As a result, they stop wanting to come visit. When this occurs, the father often accuses the mother of negatively influencing the children against him because his children no longer want to visit, when the reality is that the children don't want to feel like a guest in their father's new apartment. When he is thinking soundly and planning properly, he secures accommodations that communicate to the children that he wants them there because he has provided for them a space of their own and a place for their belongings. A home.

The final way in which depression can affect clients legally is via their interactions with me as their lawyer. When clients are immersed in depression, out of their apathy concerning the case, they often fail to communicate with me in a timely manner. However, I have deadlines by which I have to respond to the opposing lawyer, and if I miss those deadlines, the court can issue sanctions against me, my client, or both; thus, it hurts all of us! The amount of these financial sanctions is based on what the opposing lawyer charges for legal fees, so based on spending an extra (and unnecessary) two or three hours in court because of my client's lack of responsiveness, the sanction could be $300 to $1,000! Fortunately, I can go to the judge and show all of the letters that I sent to my client requesting the necessary information and avoid sanctions for myself. To my clients, this might look like I'm "ratting them out" or covering myself instead of them, but the reality is that just like I have obligations, my clients have an obligation to respond to requests in a timely manner.

Additionally, from a legal standpoint, clients' pleadings, or requests, could be affected when they are operating out of a state of depression. For example, my client might be asking for custody of the children, asking for child support, asking for more than half of the estate, etc. and have strong, justifiable reasons to expect to be granted these requests. However, if clients drag their feet or are non-responsive so that we do not respond to discovery requests in a timely manner, the court might strike these requests, saying that because we were non-responsive, we are not eligible to ask for these things in trial.

Spiritual Guidance for the Soul in the Stage of Depression

If you have been overtaken by depression, I know that nothing else seems to matter in life to you right now. I know that it takes everything you have just to be able to get out of bed – that is, if you are getting out of bed. I know that you can hardly think, because your head feels like it's in the clouds. I know that not even the best friend, closest family member, or spiritual advisor can pull you out of your funk. I know that things look really bleak right now and that they look really permanent; however, you've got to accept the fact that things will change. Don't trust me, trust God and His word. He knows what you are going through, and because He cares about you, He gives you hope that you can count on; when He says it, you can take it to the bank!

As you go through this situation, you might begin to feel as though God has abandoned you. You might wonder, "Is He angry with me?" The reality is that God is not angry with you. Even if He was, He loves you, so it would not be an anger that lasts. The bible says in Psalm 30:5, *For His anger lasts only a moment, but His favor lasts a lifetime; weeping may stay for the night, but rejoicing comes in the morning.* Many of us have heard that *weeping may endure for a night, but joy comes in the morning* so often that it has become cliché; however, it is a solid truth, because it is in Scripture! The pain that you feel will end one day, and joy will come in the morning. I once used this scripture in an attempt to encourage one of my clients, and she said that she knew that joy would come in the morning; however, she wanted to know how long the night would last. My reply to her was, "That's up to you. How long will you hold on to the past? How long will you hold on to the pain? How long will you disobey God's command to rejoice in the days that He has made and be glad in them?" You see, the period marking night and morning depend upon you, because weeping is an indication that you are reflecting on the past, but joy is an indication that you are reflecting on the future that God has in store for you! Time is one of the few things in life that you can never get back. Therefore, try not to waste too much of it looking back.

103

When joy comes in the morning, there will come a time when you no longer think of the end of your relationship and cry or fall apart. Your favorite movie and the funniest joke will make you laugh again. Seeing your best friend will bring a smile to your face again. Singing your favorite hymn will bring joy to your heart again. Spending time in prayer with God will lift your spirits and help you think clearly again. If you can just keep walking, keep moving, your tomorrow will look much brighter than your today. Joy *is* coming in the morning, and when it can begin to shine through depends on you!

James 1:2-4 gives us an encouraging word about joy that you might not have considered: *Consider it pure joy, my brothers and sisters, whenever you face trials of many kinds, because you know that the testing of your faith produces perseverance. Let perseverance finish its work so that you may be mature and complete, not lacking anything.* The bible not only tells us that God tells us to consider it joy when we face trials; it tells us that when we face these trials, you should "consider it pure joy"! *Pure joy?* The reason behind this is clear: God knows that when you go through the biggest tests and trials of our lives, if we do not allow them to break us, they can only develop us and make us stronger. They develop our strength, our resolve, our character, our patience, our ability to show restraint, our ability to show love to those who mistreat us, and ultimately, our ability to persevere! It is for this reason that we are to rejoice when we go through trials! In doing so, perseverance will do a priceless work that will result in you being more mature, more complete, and more whole than you ever thought you could be! You cannot put a price tag on such maturity and wholeness; the richest man in the world cannot pay for wholeness. Instead, it must be hard-won when God allows us to go through certain trials that test our faith and patience at their most extreme limits. Therefore, instead of allowing your trials to cause you depression, rejoice in them!

A Prayer for Direction…

Before moving on to the next chapter, pray this prayer aloud:

Lord, please deliver me from this spirit of depression. Though I have tried to snap myself out of it unsuccessfully, I am thankful that there is nothing too hard for you. I pray that Your Spirit would constantly bring back to my remembrance things that are designed to give me joy. Therefore, Lord, whenever

I am feeling down, help me to remember the joy of my salvation. Help me to remember that the joy of the Lord is my strength. As long as I am in relationship with you, regardless of what is happening around me, I have every reason in the world to have joy. Even when my mind tries to drift to negative things, I pray that you would help me to think on whatsoever things are pure, lovely, admirable, excellent, and praiseworthy so that I can be joyous in my spirit and mindful to bless you at all times. I thank You, Lord, that each day that I reflect upon Your goodness, depression is leaving me, and one day I shall rejoice in your presence with no depression at all!

Amen!

CHAPTER SEVEN

The Stage of Acceptance:
"Okay… This Is My *New* Real Life Now!"

The fifth and final stage of loss and grief is the stage of acceptance. After surviving all of the denial, anger, bargaining, and depression, this is the stage in which a person finally stops struggling with what has happened, why it happened, whose fault it was, and how the situation can be fixed. Instead of being preoccupied with hashing and re-hashing these questions on a daily basis, the person now accepts that the reality that he or she is living life as it is currently. *This is my real life now… and it's not so bad!*

Once people reach the stage of acceptance, they are no longer looking backward; they are ready to move forward. Life is now about adjusting to a new context, developing new routines, building a life as a single person, learning how to live in contentment without their spouse, and looking forward to the great things that lay ahead in the future. No longer are they filled with pessimism, desperation, or bitterness. Instead, they are filled with optimism, hope, and – usually by this point – some level of forgiveness. *Regardless of whose fault it was, it happened, it was unfortunate, and it's over now, so it's time for me to move on!*

I can really appreciate clients who have done the work on themselves to the point that they have made it to this stage of loss and grief – and it does take work! Getting to the stage of acceptance is not something that passively happens. In order to get here, people must really face themselves, be willing to evaluate their role in what happened, be courageous enough to ask hard questions about themselves for which the answers might not be so pretty, be brave enough to embrace an uncertain future, and most of all, have the audacity to forgive themselves as well as others and still maintain a sense of peace and contentment.

Navigating the other stages of loss and grief and getting to the stage of acceptance takes a longer time for some, a shorter time for others.

However, it's not about how long it takes to get there – it's just about getting there. If you can't reach this stage quickly with class and grace, strive to reach it with whatever bumps, bruises, and battle scars you need; just strive to reach the goal. Once you get to acceptance, not only will your life be much more satisfying and fulfilling, but your divorce case will flow that much more smoothly.

My mind flashes back to an older client of mine, a woman who had been married to her husband for 42 years and shared with whom she shared three beautiful children. I vividly recall that she was such a beautiful woman in spirit, personality, and demeanor when I first met her in my office for a consultation. She was very straightforward, saying that her husband had left her and moved in with another woman. She never thought that this would have happened to her, but it had, and she had made peace with the idea and accepted it as her *current* reality. At this point, she just wanted to get the divorce over and done. Her husband had already filed for the divorce on his own; he was pro se and representing himself in court. It tickled me that she had no respect for the fact that he had not hired a lawyer to handle his business. She would say, "He sent me some rag tag pieces of paper saying that he wanted a divorce!" However, she was determined to hire a lawyer to ensure that her divorce was done right; she wanted to be sure that when it was over, it was really over and that the court would not reject the submitted paperwork. During the process, her husband was resistant; he didn't want to yield on any issue. Despite this, she did not disparage her husband, or speak of him negatively as she did his choice to pursue the divorce without the help of counsel. She truly loved her husband, but she was not about to beg him to stay in their marriage. This woman stayed calm the whole time, handling the situation matter-of-factly with such grace and class. She gave me no problems at all and was the ideal client. In fact, I was more devastated than she was over the end of their 42year union!

It is a rarity for clients to start the divorce process with such a sense of acceptance. However, it is not rare for them to reach this stage at some point between the initial consultation and the actual court date, which can take anywhere from 60 days to two years. It takes them a moment to get there, but they do arrive.

For example, I had a client who was actually a corporate executive that practiced law. When she first found out about her husband's cheating, she was an absolute wreck! She had lots of reasons to be angry, including the fact his girlfriend was about to have a baby, and they weren't even divorced yet. As a result, in the beginning, my client was so angry, bitter, and sad that she wanted to destroy her husband! She brought boxes and boxes of documents to my office because she wanted to mount the strongest case possible against him in this fight. However, by the time we got to court and were getting ready to finalize the divorce, she had accepted her situation, and she was at peace. In fact, when she walked into the courtroom, she looked me square in the eyes and simply said, "I am ready." By this time, her husband and his attorney came ready for an all-out battle; after all, we had both done extensive discovery, submitted massive amounts of documents, and exchanged lots of angry letters. Her words floored them: "I am at peace. He is our child's father. I don't want to fight anymore. I am ready for this to be done, and I just want to settle." As a result of this completely unexpected turn, we settled the case that morning, we proved up the case before the court, she was granted the child support she wanted, the car she wanted, and the property division she wanted. In fact, her settlement was pretty close to what she would have demanded if they had fought things out in court. She got everything she wanted and I believe one of the reasons for this was because she was at peace. The divorce process was harsh while she worked through her different stages of loss and grief, but because she ended up at acceptance, the ending was an easy one.

While some people start the divorce process already having entered into the stage of acceptance and others reach this stage somewhere between the start of the divorce and its finalization, there are others who go all the way through the process and do not find this sense of acceptance until the divorce is complete. This is understandable, because at that point, whether they have accepted their situation or not, the divorce is finished. Where they could not find their own sense of finality to move on to acceptance, the final divorce decree with the signature of the judge makes it final for all involved. This can prompt them, for the very first time, to really, truly accept where their relationship is: over.

I can remember one client bringing a case to me, the likes of which I had never encountered before: she had met an immigrant when she was in college and he was in graduate school, they "fell in love", and they got married – right as his student visa was about to expire. For her, this was a full marriage; she did all of the things a wife would do to build a home and care for her husband and she was fulfilled and quite happy. However, she later discovered that he had an entire family back in his homeland, including a wife, kids, a house, and numerous assets. She was devastated beyond belief. She cried constantly when she would come to my office to meet with me, not only because her hopes of the fantasy life with the dream house, the white picket fence, the kids, and the life in the suburbs with the perfect husband were dashed, but because she felt so used by the man she had married. When it was almost time for the trial, she called me and said she didn't think she could bear seeing him, so she couldn't go to court. I told her that she had to go, and I assured her that she had done nothing wrong and that the judge was almost certainly going to give her what she wanted given the deception she had endured. Still, she was very reluctant. The day of the trial, she called me from the lobby of the courthouse paralyzed with fear; she said she couldn't come up to the courtroom. After I told her to hold tight, I went to get her, encouraging her that she was safe and to be strong. Once we finally made our way into the courtroom together, we looked around: her "husband" was nowhere to be found. Despite his absence, we moved forward with the divorce proceedings. The judge gave her a really good settlement; however, it came with a disclaimer. He said, "Ma'am, I am so sorry this happened to you. This is not the first time I have seen this. Everything I am giving you, you will probably never be able to get, because all of his assets are in another country. In any case, you deserve all of this and more." I was moved. I turned to look at my client, and at first, she looked like a deer caught in the headlights. Then, right before our very eyes, a transformation occurred. It was as if we could literally see a light going off in her mind as this exhilarated look came across her face and she asked, "So am I divorced?" The judge said, "Yes!" She asked, "Am I free?" Again, the judge replied, "Yes!" Then, she looked at me and exclaimed, "I'm free! I am freeeee!" I had never witnessed anything like this before. At this, she finally exhaled. She relaxed. She accepted her situation, she was finally at peace, and the man she once believed to be her husband no longer had a hold on her. She was on cloud nine and practically skipped out of the courtroom, exclaiming, "It's done! It's done!" No one in the courtroom could stop smiling as we watched this woman celebrate the fact that the chains had been broken, and she was free and finally at peace.

What Does a Client in the Acceptance Stage Look Like?

As one can imagine, lawyers love dealing with clients who have reached the acceptance stage. If clients are not at the point of acceptance during the initial consultation, their lawyers at least hope that they will reach this stage at some point during the process so that the case can proceed smoothly and make things easier for everyone. When clients are in the acceptance stage:

- They are more calm and peaceful.

- When they come for appointments, they are all about business.

- They do not use their time telling emotional stories. In fact, when they talk about how they ended up needing a divorce, they do so very flatly with little to no emotion – just the facts.

- They are alert, attentive, and very present during their meetings with the lawyer.

- They do not use their lawyer as a therapist; instead, they relate to them as they would to any other professional like a bank teller or a clerk at the dry cleaners.

- They tend to be upbeat when they arrive for appointments and exchange pleasantries ("Good morning! How are you?") and observe business etiquette.

111

- They tend to be very level-headed and not overly-demanding of their lawyer.

- They tend to be very informed and sharp as they think through their process and develop a strategy.

When clients are in the acceptance stage, they are no longer operating out of emotion. Instead, they are operating as rational, soundthinking, level-headed clients who are simply trying to get the divorce done and settled once and for all. These are the clients who are not willing to fight as much as clients who are operating out of other stages. Clients in the acceptance stage are usually quite generous when it comes to accepting proposals; they refuse to fight over pennies, kitchen utensils, or even pets. After all, they understand, these things can easily be replaced. As a result of their high level of cooperation, their divorces generally cost less.

The Legal Advantages of Operating from a Point of Acceptance

You will notice that while operating out of other stages is wrought with disadvantages, there are no legal disadvantages when operating from a point of acceptance – only advantages. For example, the first advantage has already been mentioned: divorces cost less once you have accepted your situation. Divorces can cost time, money, and emotional capital, and you can save all three when you operate from a place of emotional peace. Nothing but good can come out of this!

Another advantage of operating from a point of acceptance during divorce is that your children can greatly benefit. When both parents are at peace throughout the divorce process, they do not force their children to choose between which of their parents to love. Instead, the children can freely love each parent equally because both parents are showing mutual respect for one another.

There's one particular family that I know of that exemplifies two parents working together for the benefit of their children with model behavior. I know of their story not because they were my clients, but because they live in my neighborhood, and our children are friends. My first interaction was with their son. I was acting as the taxi cab driver that day as their son and my son were in the back seat. I heard my son ask their son, "Who do you like best: your mom or your dad?" My curiosity was piqued, so I turned down the radio volume a bit to hear his response. To this, their son answered, "I love them both! They are both great parents!" I smiled to myself at hearing this. Out of the mouth of babes!

Actually, despite the question (I thought my son was asking because he had been disciplined and was angry with one of us), my husband and I both thought that his parents were married until we found out differently via a fluke. My husband had carpool duty after dance practice one day, so he dropped their daughter off at a home in the neighborhood. However, the next time he had carpool duty after dance practice, he was taking her to the same house, and she said, "No! I have to be dropped off at my mom's house today!" Following her directions, he took her to the other house, only to find out that they were a divorced family. Yet, both the mom and dad lived in the same neighborhood in such close proximity that their children could ride their bicycles between the two houses! Operating from a place of peace and acceptance, they decided to release their offenses with one another and do what was best for the children.

At another time, I saw both the mother and the father at a dance recital. They were sitting together with their children in between them and interacting like one big happy family! What a great example of what can be accomplished when two parents keep what is most important – the children – at the forefront and bury the hatchet so that they can work together!

Spiritual Guidance for the Soul in the Stage of Acceptance

If you have reached the stage of acceptance in your journey through loss and grief, you have already done well! All you can do from this point is grow, grow, grow! *Grow in what?* you might ask. Grow in courage! Grow in confidence! Grow in Christ!

Your future is so bright, not only in natural things but in spiritual things! In the natural, you will find that your new life offers you so many opportunities for growth, development, and progression that you have never experienced before, so take advantage of them!

In the Spirit, Romans 8:18 says, *I consider that our present sufferings are not worth comparing with the glory that will be revealed in us!* Thus, though it might seem like what you are going through today is a big thing, when you compare it to what God has for you in the future, it pales in comparison! If God allowed your divorce to happen, He is going to do just as Romans 8:28 says: *And we know that in all things God works for the good of those who love Him, who have been called according to His purpose.* God will take this thing that you look at as a "bad thing" or the "worst thing that has ever happened to you in your life" and allow it to be used to produce something good – something great – in your life. Just wait and see! Jeremiah 29:11 also encourages us by telling us that God has a plan for our lives: *"For I know the plans I have for you," declares the Lord, "plans to prosper you and not to harm you, plans to give you hope and a future."* Despite how things look or feel at this moment, know that God still has plans for you, and these plans are greater than you can even imagine! However, He cannot reveal His plans for you if you stay stuck and bogged down in your grief. You must let go of the past and open your heart to embrace what He has for you – hope and a glorious future!

Finally, you might be one who says, "I know God's word is true, but I'll believe all of this when I see it!" This is all good and fine, but keep in mind that the bible says in John 20:29, *"...blessed are those who have not seen and yet have believed.*" Do you have to see everything to believe it first, or can you trust God at His word and believe that what He says He will do, He will do? Are you able to do as the bible says in 2 Corinthians 5:7 and *"walk by faith and not by sight"*? I guarantee that if you do, you will be rewarded! Hebrews 11:6 says, *"...without faith it is impossible to please God, because anyone who comes to Him must believe that He exists and that He rewards those who earnestly seek Him."* If you can be faithful to believe, the Lord will reward you with a future richer than that which you could ever imagine!

A Prayer for Direction...

Before moving on to the next chapter, pray this prayer aloud:

Lord, thank You for taking me through this process of grief and allowing me to get to the point of acceptance. I am grateful to You for the peace that comes along with truly embracing where I am and what has happened. I rest in Your sovereignty, because whatever has happened only happened because You allowed it to happen to shape who I am to become. Because You know best, Lord, I rest in everything that You allow. I pray that You would help me to continue to walk by faith and not by sight, because this is the only way to please You. Thank You, Lord, for delivering me, for the destiny that You have prepared for me, and for joy, for the morning has come! Amen!

CHAPTER EIGHT

The Final Piece to Wholeness:
Walking in Step with God

At this point in the process, you should feel more equipped to understand what to expect in a divorce both legally and emotionally. There's a lot to remember, a lot to do, and a lot to be mindful of – but you can do it! However, while following my advice and heeding my insights might help you keep things under control in the natural throughout your divorce process, if you do not have your life together spiritually, you could still find yourself in a very challenging place.

Having a relationship with God is of utmost importance throughout one's entire life – not just in a divorce. You see, while information can touch a man's mind, only God can touch a man's spirit and give him a peace so deep that even his mind cannot comprehend. While man can have a tough mind that causes him to behave in a strong and confident manner, this strength is limited; only God can provide him with the fullness of joy, and this joy of the Lord will be his strength. Man's might, strength and power are limited; however, God tells us that when we are weak, this is the point where He is made strong in our lives.

Many people in today's day and age operate out of a sense of rugged individualism, self-reliance, and independence. This mindset causes them to lean and depend only upon themselves, to trust no one, to never ask for help, and to go at things all on their own. What a lonely and vulnerable way to live – especially in the midst of a tragedy like divorce. God desires to us to have a relationship with Him that is so reliant that we acknowledge that we cannot get through the situation without Him. He wants us to be so dependent upon Him that we consult Him before every decision, before taking any action, and even before we allow ourselves to think or feel certain things. He wants to be everything to us throughout this process: our joy, our strength, our counselor, our helper, our provider, our advisor, our confidante, our sounding board... our best friend!

If you already have a relationship with God, you already undoubtedly talk to Him, allow Him speak to you through His Word in the Bible, live your life according to His will, and rest in His care and comfort daily. However, allow me to give you a little spiritual advice that will help you move more smoothly through your divorce process.

Pray in your *own* way.

Perhaps you are not the most "religious" of people, or perhaps you are. Regardless of whether you are or not, when you are at such a critical crossroads in your life, you need to be able to talk to God your way in your own words! This is the time to toss the "religious speak" and the flowery language out of the window and really talk to God. Don't try to pray like you hear the people pray over the pulpit at church. Don't try to pray like you hear the preachers on television pray, using phrases and concepts that you hardly understand. Pray like you are at the feet of a King making requests to Him that will save your life, and don't be hesitant to pray for yourself!

For example, now is the time to trade in the "Thou hast been a Wonderful Counselor in mine eyes and hast the might to deliver thine servant from the hand of the evil one," for "God, you know I am hurting like heck and I'm confused about what to do, so I need you to please, please, *please* give me direction! Please tell me what to do and where to go and when to do it so that I don't make decisions that will destroy myself! Protect me from the devil, because I am so vulnerable right now, and please do not let him take me out!" Cry out to God for help like you would cry out to your best friend, and watch Him come through!

Pray without ceasing.

1 Thessalonians 5:17 tells us to "Pray without ceasing" or "Pray continually". Throughout the divorce process, you will need to be in constant communication with God about what to do, when to do it, and how to do it. When you are in a right relationship with Him and ask Him

for this guidance, He will answer. As your loving Father, He cares about you, so the answers that He provides are never meant to destroy you – only to develop you and drive you into His will for your life.

In Luke 18:1, Jesus said that "Men always ought to pray and not lose heart". This is an encouragement to always maintain your connection with God through prayer in this process, and because you are constantly in communication with Him, you will not grow weary or lose heart. Practically speaking, one might wonder how a person can "pray without ceasing" or "always pray" in the midst of busy careers, taking care of children, and tending to the daily business of life. The answer is simple: we are to be in a posture of prayer in which our spirit is tuned in to God's voice so that we can hear Him in the midst of whatever we are doing. This way, as we are walking from the parking lot into the grocery store, we can speak to Him in our heart, and He can speak back. While we are watching the kids' soccer practice, we can speak to Him in our heart, and He can speak back. While you're writing an e-mail to your spouse regarding the divorce, you can speak to Him, and He can speak back. While we are on the treadmill getting in a few miles, standing in the shower, or boarding the airplane, we can speak to Him in our heart, and He can speak back.

Praying without ceasing, therefore, means more than having a dedicated time of prayer in the morning before you start your busy day. Instead, it means maintaining a constant, ongoing connection with God throughout the day wherein you are always tapped into His spiritual frequency and listening for His voice and His prompting. No matter how busy the hustle and bustle gets around you, you can hear His voice, and He can hear yours!

Pray openly and honestly.

Hebrews 4:13 tells us that "Nothing in all creation is hidden from God's sight. Everything is uncovered and laid bare before the eyes of Him to whom we must give an account." Earlier on, I advised you to have the courage to be honest with yourself about what you want and honest with your attorney about what you want, even if you think that there is no chance of getting what you want. Now, I am advising you to be honest with God about what you want. After all, this scripture tells us that He already knows; He is just waiting for you to ask, and if it is His will, He will grant it to you!

The bible also tells us in Hebrews 4:16 that we can go "boldly to the throne of grace, that we may obtain mercy and find grace to help in time of need." God is the merciful and gracious King, sitting on His throne, waiting to hear your petitions and provide help in this time of need. Therefore, ask for what you want. If you want reconciliation, be bold enough to ask for it. If you want full custody of the children, ask for it. If these things are in His will for your life, He will do it. If they are not in His will for your life, accept that He knows best, and praise Him for His infinite wisdom. James 4:2 says that "...You have not, because you ask not". This suggests that there are certain things that God desires to grant in our lives, but because we did not ask for them in prayer, He did not give them to us. Therefore, when you pray, always ask for what you want! If it's yours to have according to the will of God, it will happen.

Another thing that you must be brutally honest about is your role in the divorce. In a divorce, no one person carries 100% of the blame for the dissolution of the marriage; at some level, both parties played a part. Perhaps you committed adultery, or perhaps you were the one who was cheated on by your spouse. Perhaps you drove the household's finances into the red with your compulsive shopping or lack of financial discipline, or perhaps you were the one who discovered your spouse's out-of-control spending habits only after you found out that you were in debt over your heads. Perhaps you stopped allowing your partner to be intimate with you, or perhaps you stopped trying to be intimate with your partner.

Regardless of what role you played, you played some role at some level. For most people, the role they played brings a certain level of guilt that they do not even dare to share with their best friend. However, you do not need to carry this burden alone; you can share it with God. Nothing is hidden from God's sight, so try as you may, you can never hide anything from Him. God is omniscient – all-knowing – so not only did He see what you did all the time that you were doing it, He knew how it was going to affect the relationship and how ultimately, it would contribute to the dissolution of the marriage. In fact, the reality is that God knew that you were going to do it before you did it! Your behavior was a surprise to you because you didn't know that you were going to do it, but because He is omniscient, He wasn't surprised at all; in fact, He expected it.

Therefore, be willing to lay it all down before God. He's God, so he's seen everything that has happened on this earth since the beginning of time. Consequently, nothing is too terrible, too risqué, too abominable, or too shameful for you to confess. Don't sugarcoat anything, because He already knows the truth. Dare to speak words about your behavior that you have never spoken before. Dare to make yourself articulate confessions that you promised would go with you to the grave. Confessing everything that you did to contribute to the divorce will bring such a sense of relief, such a catharsis, and such a sense of peace that when you finish, I guarantee that you'll feel better. You'll feel lighter. You'll feel more at peace. There's a reason for this! Proverbs 28:13 says that "Whoever conceals their sins does not prosper, but the one who confesses and renounces them finds mercy". Open confession is good for the soul, so release it, and then ask for His mercy! Because you are His, surely, you will receive it.

Pray with or for a forgiving heart.

Mark 11:25-26 says, "And when you stand praying, if you hold anything against anyone, forgive them, so that your Father in heaven may forgive you your sins. But if you do not forgive, neither will your Father in heaven forgive your sins." When we pray, we must pray with a forgiving heart; this scripture tells us that our relationship with God depends on it! No matter how spiritual you are, you are not immune to the attacks of the enemy that tell you that your spouse has done something that is not forgivable. However, we must remember that as sons and daughters of God, we are forgiven, and it is our duty and responsibility to extend this same forgiveness to others, regardless of what they have done. Just as our heavenly father forgives us for anything and everything we do when we violate Him, so must we forgive those who wrong or violate us. If we do not, we do not hurt them; we hurt ourselves and our relationship with God!

Many people think that forgiveness is a process that should take as much time as they need it to take, but consider this: in 1 John 1:9, God says that "If we confess our sins, He is faithful and just to forgive our sins and cleans us from all unrighteousness." How quickly does God forgive? He does it quickly – immediately! How quickly should we forgive? The same way! Forgiveness is something that you must will yourself to do. When you are a believer who is having a hard time forgiving, it is because you are having a hard time letting go of your will and embracing God's will. The process that you are going through is that of overcoming your disobedience to God, not one of healing that will result in forgiveness. To forgive is to pardon someone for a wrong done to you. It costs you only obedience to biblical principles and letting go of your pride – nothing else.

Perhaps you are struggling with having a forgiving heart. Perhaps you feel so hurt and so wronged by your spouse that you feel like releasing them would let them off of the hook too easily for the wrong that they committed. Perhaps you are not seeking to forgive them, but you are seeking vengeance upon them, even though Romans 12:19 says, "Beloved, do not avenge yourselves, but rather give place to wrath; for it is written, 'Vengeance is Mine, I will repay,' says the Lord." If you are in this situation, find a brother or sister in Christ that is willing to pray with you and for you to have a forgiving heart. Without a heart of forgiveness, you will be the one that pays the penalty and the one whose relationship with God will suffer.

One might ask, "How can I forgive someone who is still currently doing wrong to me?" The answer to this is simple, because it's right there in the bible. Proverbs 25:21-22 says, "If your enemy is hungry, give him bread to eat, and if he is thirsty, give him water to drink; for so you will heap coals of fire on his head, and the Lord will reward you." Also, Luke 6:28 says to "bless those who curse you and pray for those who mistreat you"! In other words, these scriptures are saying to kill them with kindness! Again, if this is something that you are struggling with, pray for obedience to Scripture. Only by walking in God's love and forgiveness can you experience the fullness of life that He has for you!

Pray for strength and protection.

Ephesians 6:10 says, "Finally, be strong in the Lord and in His mighty power." Also, Nehemiah 8:10 reminds us, "The joy of the Lord is your strength." As you can probably tell, divorce can be brutal. During this process, you will need all of the supernatural strength you can possibly access in order to hold things together and maintain a sense of peace. If you've witnessed even a few people go through divorce, you can testify that divorce can break even the strongest person down financially, emotionally, mentally and physically. Divorce can be a big drain, so it is important to access extra sources of strength during this period. Pray that the Lord would strengthen you with His mighty power. When you are feeling weak, emotionally exhausted, and at your wit's end, the Lord will come through and make you strong!

It is also important during time to pray for protection. Everyone tends to feel a little unstable and vulnerable when a family is broken apart and everyone no longer lives under the same roof. The enemy would love to come in and prey on the family in such a state, so it is important to constantly pray for the protection of the Lord. The bible tells us in Job 1:10 that the Lord is able to put a hedge around us and our families so that we are protected from the attacks of the enemy: "Have you not put a hedge around him and his household and everything he has?" Therefore, pray that the Lord would offer this protection for you and your family. When you have to adjust to living without a man in house, which used to offer a certain measure of peace and security, pray for protection. When you have to adjust to living without a woman in the house that offers nurturing and covering, pray for protection. When you send your children off for weekend visits with the other parent, pray for protection. When you are dealing with an angry, irate spouse whose behavior seems out of control and unpredictable, pray for protection. The Lord will indeed be a fence around you!

Pray for a sound mind.

2 Timothy 1:7 says, "For God has not given us a spirit of fear, but of love, power, and a sound mind." Throughout the five stages of grief, I repeatedly referred to the importance of knowing where you are in the process so that you can determine whether you are making decisions out of your emotional state versus operating out of a sound mind. If you find yourself constantly operating out of your emotions, pray that God would give you soundness of mind. This is critical, because the decisions that you

make during the divorce process will be decisions that will impact your quality of life for the rest of your life! Thus, you must be thinking soundly!

Also, you can expect during the divorce process to receive LOTS of advice, recommendations, and information from very well-meaning people in your life. They will offer their two-cents of what to do, how to do it, where to go, how to act with your spouse, how to deal with your attorney, what strategies to use, etc. Be careful to not take everyone's advice and run with it; it might sound good, but it might not be God's will for your life. Instead, seek God for wisdom and a sound mind before acting upon anything that you hear. In fact, James 1:5 says, "If any of you lacks wisdom, let him ask of God, who gives to all liberally and without reproach, and it will be given to him." Your loved ones truly do mean well, but only God knows the true direction in which you should go!

Pray for wholeness.

James 1:4 tells us what God desires for us: "But let patience have its perfect work, that you may be perfect and complete, lacking nothing." Another way of saying "perfect and complete, lacking nothing" is wholeness! As I explained earlier in the book, it is very difficult to determine who has won or lost in a divorce. Both parties must endure so much pain, so much grief, and so much loss, that most of the time, it seems as if there are never any real winners. However, if I had to classify a win/lose in divorce, I would have to say that sometimes, the winner is just the one who is made whole – the one who can walk away from the process with mind, body, and spirit intact, perfect and complete, lacking nothing. Delivered! The scripture tells us that this is God's will for your life, so be bold enough to pray for it. Ask God to make you whole to the point where you feel that you are lacking nothing, and watch Him do it!

Work through a devotional.

Psalm 1:2 tells us that we will be blessed if our "delight is in the law of the Lord" and meditate in it day and night. During the process of divorce, it is important that you keep God's word before you day and night. Before you get started with the busyness of your day in the morning, take a few moments to read a scripture or two and then quietly mediate on it so that you get your mind on God. Write down your reflections. Establishing this connection early on will make getting through the day much easier. Then, at night, before you go to bed, read some scriptures again, and then meditate on them. Doing this will help you to have a sweet, peaceful night's rest as you reflect upon the goodness of God and how He is continually keeping you throughout this process.

What If I Don't Have a Relationship with God?

All of the principles that I teach concerning spirituality are based on Christianity, which is characterized by accepting the sacrifice of Jesus Christ on the cross for our sins. If you don't' already have a relationship with God, you are missing out on the love, joy, peace, forgiveness, and righteousness that being in right relationship with the Creator of the universe has to offer. He is the only God, and the only way to Him is through accepting His Son, Jesus Christ, whom He sent to earth to die on the cross so that the sins of all who accept Him would be forgiven.

In order to enter into a relationship with the Lord Jesus Christ, you must acknowledge the following:

- Adam, the first man that God created, sinned against God in the Garden of Eden and became a sinner. Because Adam was the federal and seminal head of all humanity, all who were born after him were born sinners.

- Your sin nature makes you a sinner in need of salvation. Because God cannot look upon sin, our fellowship and communication with God are broken as a result of our sinfulness.

- The wages of sin is death, so our sin nature makes us worthy of death, which is physical separation from God in eternity.

- God sent His Son, Jesus Christ, to earth to die for us so that we could receive salvation. Jesus was both fully God and fully man.

- Jesus lived a sinless life on earth; though He was tempted, and He did not sin, and He never violated the Law.

- Even though He was innocent, Jesus died in our place. Even though He never sinned, He became sin so that through His death on the cross, we did not have to die for ourselves. Instead, we (sinful humanity) could become righteous by accepting His death on the cross.

- Jesus died an actual death, but after three days, the Holy Spirit raised Him from the dead. After this, He ascended into heaven, where He now sits at the right hand of God and lives to intercede on our behalf.

- If we confess with our mouth the Lord Jesus and believe in our heart that God raised Him from the dead, we shall be saved and have eternal life with Him.

Do you believe these things? If you do, you can be saved! Simply pray the following prayer out loud and invite Jesus Christ into your heart:

Lord, I confess to You I am a sinner. I know that sin separates me from You. I now ask You to forgive my sins. I know that Jesus died for me on the cross and will take my sin away if I believe in Him. Jesus, I do believe in You. I ask You to come into my life (heart) and give me eternal life. Thank You so much for forgiving me and giving me eternal life. Amen![IV]

Congratulations! Now that you have believed in the principles of salvation and invited the Lord to come into your life, you are genuinely saved! You are a believer! Next, you should seek out a local Christian church that espouses the beliefs that are outlined above and join yourself with them. They will ensure that you grow and learn more about your faith and how to walk in a peaceful, loving, holistic relationship with the Lord Jesus Christ!

[IV] Prayer Source: http://www.fbchsv.org/796758

A Prayer for Direction…

As you conclude this chapter, pray this prayer aloud:

Lord, thank You for Your love, Your goodness, Your tender mercy, Your loving kindness, Your guidance, Your wisdom, and Your direction! Thank You for being such an awesome healer, an awesome provider, and an awesome deliverer! Thank you for taking me through this book, helping me to understand the legal process of divorce, enlightening me on what to expect throughout the process, opening my eyes to vulnerabilities, and preparing me for the road ahead. Thank You also for the promise that You will be with me throughout the whole process. You already know what the outcome will be, so regardless of what You allow it to be, I will accept it and rest knowing that Your hand was in the midst of it. Thank You for being so faithful, even at the times when I have been faithless. Thank you for filling my heart with Your love, joy, and peace through one of the most difficult experiences I will ever encounter. Most of all, God, thank You for the testimony that I will have and the testimony that my life will be as a result of coming through this process with my sanity, my stability, and my spirit intact. I love You, Lord! Praise Your holy name! Amen!

ABOUT THE AUTHOR

Ronique Bastine Robinson is board certified in family law by the Texas Board of Legal Specialization. An attorney for over 20 years, an adjunct law professor, a municipal judge and a public speaker. During her extensive legal career she has represented thousands of clients as a specialist in a wide range of family law matters. Robinson is highly sought after by many due to her ability to practically navigate clients through both the complex legalities of divorce as well as through the emotional journey accompanying the process. Judge Robinson serves on several state boards and law commissions and generously donates her time and legal expertise to her church as well as to a number of other civic and non-profit organizations. She resides in Houston, Texas with her husband and three children.

16002563R00086

Made in the USA
San Bernardino, CA
14 October 2014